PEARSON
my World GEOGRAPHY

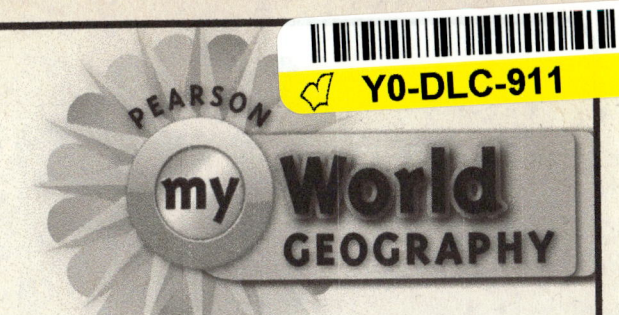

ASSESSMENT HANDBOOK

IN PRINT AND ONLINE AT
myworldgeography.com

- Includes two assessments for every chapter
- Provides rubrics to establish criteria for assessment
- Helps monitor adequate yearly progress using benchmark tests
- Prepares students for end-of-course exams

PEARSON

Boston, Massachusetts
Chandler, Arizona
Glenview, Illinois
Upper Saddle River, New Jersey

Copyright © **Pearson Education, Inc., or its affiliates.** All Rights Reserved. Printed in the United States of America. This publication is protected by copyright, and permission should be obtained from the publisher prior to any prohibited reproduction, storage in a retrieval system, or transmission in any form or by any means, electronic, mechanical, photocopying, recording, or likewise. The publisher hereby grants permission to reproduce the test-taking strategies, assessment rubrics, chapter tests, and course practice tests, in part or in whole, for classroom use only, the number not to exceed the number of students in each class. Notice of copyright must appear on all copies. For information regarding permissions, write to Pearson Curriculum Group Rights & Permissions, One Lake Street, Upper Saddle River, New Jersey 07458.

Pearson, Prentice Hall, Pearson Prentice Hall, and myWorld Geography are trademarks, in the U.S. and/or other countries, of Pearson Education, Inc., or its affiliates.

PEARSON

ISBN-13: 978-0-13-363801-1
ISBN-10: 0-13-363801-4

6 7 8 9 10 V056 14 13

Contents

Test-Taking Strategies... 1
Rubrics... 7

Core Concepts
Part 1: Tools of Geography
Test A.. 13
Test B.. 15
Part 2: Our Planet, Earth
Test A.. 17
Test B.. 19
Part 3: Climates and Ecosystems
Test A.. 21
Test B.. 23
Part 4: Human-Environment Interaction
Test A.. 25
Test B.. 27
Part 5: Economics and Geography
Test A.. 29
Test B.. 31
Part 6: Population and Movement
Test A.. 33
Test B.. 35
Part 7: Culture and Geography
Test A.. 37
Test B.. 39
Part 8: Government and Citizenship
Test A.. 41
Test B.. 43
Part 9: Tools of History
Test A.. 45
Test B.. 47

Chapter 1 The United States
Test A.. 49
Test B.. 51
Chapter 2 Canada
Test A.. 53
Test B.. 55
Chapter 3 Mexico
Test A.. 57
Test B.. 59
Chapter 4 Central America and the Caribbean
Test A.. 61
Test B.. 63
Chapter 5 Caribbean South America
Test A.. 65
Test B.. 67
Chapter 6 The Andes and the Pampas
Test A.. 69
Test B.. 71
Chapter 7 Brazil
Test A.. 73
Test B.. 75

Copyright © Pearson Education, Inc., or its affiliates. All Rights Reserved.

Contents

Chapter 8 Ancient and Medieval Europe
Test A...77
Test B...79

Chapter 9 Europe in Modern Times
Test A...81
Test B...83

Chapter 10 Western Europe
Test A...85
Test B...87

Chapter 11 Eastern Europe
Test A...89
Test B...91

Chapter 12 Russia
Test A...93
Test B...95

Chapter 13 West and Central Africa
Test A...97
Test B...99

Chapter 14 Southern and Eastern Africa
Test A..101
Test B..103

Chapter 15 North Africa
Test A..105
Test B..107

Chapter 16 Arabia and Iraq
Test A..109
Test B..111

Chapter 17 Israel and Its Neighbors
Test A..113
Test B..115

Chapter 18 Iran, Turkey, and Cyprus
Test A..117
Test B..119

Chapter 19 Central Asia and the Caucasus
Test A..121
Test B..123

Chapter 20 South Asia
Test A..125
Test B..127

Chapter 21 China and Its Neighbors
Test A..129
Test B..131

Chapter 22 Japan and the Koreas
Test A..133
Test B..135

Chapter 23 Southeast Asia
Test A..137
Test B..139

Chapter 24 Australia and the Pacific
Test A..141
Test B..143

Final Test..145

Answer Key..161

Copyright © Pearson Education, Inc., or its affiliates. All Rights Reserved.

Name _____ Class _____ Date _____

Analyzing Multiple-Choice Questions

Multiple-choice questions can be tricky, so be sure to read the question and all of the answer choices before you choose the best answer. These five steps can help you answer a multiple-choice question correctly.

Steps for Analyzing a Multiple-Choice Question

STEP 1 Carefully read the stem. Read through the entire question before choosing an answer.

STEP 2 Note key words, clues, or absolutes in the question or stem. Identify any key words that can be used as clues. Identify any absolutes, and note how they limit possible answers.

STEP 3 Read *all* the possible answers carefully. Read each possible answer for words or phrases that make it incorrect.

STEP 4 Eliminate answers that are obviously wrong. Narrow your list of possible choices.

STEP 5 Select the choice that correctly answers the question or completes the statement. The best answers should be a complete and accurate response to the stem.

Quick Tip
Be sure to read the entire question before choosing an answer.

Answer the following questions using the steps to analyze multiple-choice questions. Write your answers on a separate sheet of paper.

1. As feudalism ended and trade increased, Europe found itself in a time of renewed interest in art and learning, called the
   A Catholic Reformation.
   B Inquisition.
   C Renaissance.
   D Reformation.

2. Thomas Newcomen and James Watt both invented
   A electric light bulbs.
   B gravity detectors.
   C navigation instruments.
   D steam engines.

3. Which king believed so strongly in absolutism that he said, "L'état, c'est moi"?
   A Louis XIV of France
   B Philip II of Spain
   C King Augustus II of Poland
   D Henry VIII of England

4. Which countries were members of the Axis Powers during World War II?
   A the United States, Germany, and France
   B Japan, Italy, and Britain
   C Britain, France, and the United States
   D Germany, Italy, and Japan

Test-Taking Strategies

Copyright © Pearson Education, Inc., or its affiliates. All Rights Reserved.

Name _____ Class _____ Date _____

Identifying the Main Idea in a Reading Passage

Good readers are like detectives. They look for clues that reveal the main idea of a passage. The main idea is the message the writer wants you to remember. Learn how to recognize the main idea of a reading passage before answering test questions by following these steps.

Steps for Identifying the Main Idea in a Reading Passage

STEP 1 Read the title of the passage. The title often gives you an idea of what the passage is about.

STEP 2 Identify the topic sentence. Skim the passage to find the topic sentence, which often appears at the beginning or end of a passage.

STEP 3 Read the passage carefully. Pay close attention to what it says.

STEP 4 Identify supporting details. Notice how the details relate to the topic sentence.

STEP 5 Write one sentence that states the main idea in your own words. Make sure your main idea statement relates to all of the supporting details.

Quick Tip
Skimming means reading quickly while looking for key words that indicate time, cause-and-effect relationships, or comparisons.

Read the following passage. Use the steps to identify the main idea of the passage. Then write one sentence that states the main idea in your own words on a separate sheet of paper.

British Government

You have read about King John signing the Magna Carta in 1215. This document limited the power of the king and gave rights to his people. It was the beginning of democratic government in England. Today, the British government is a constitutional monarchy. This means the monarch is the ceremonial leader, but Parliament makes the laws. Unlike the U.S. Constitution, the British constitution is not a single document, but a group of laws and court decisions. The ceremonial leader is Queen Elizabeth II, who serves as a symbol of Britain's nationhood.

Copyright © Pearson Education, Inc., or its affiliates. All Rights Reserved.

Name _____ Class _____ Date _____

Understanding and Interpreting Bar Graphs

Some test questions require you to read a bar graph. A bar graph is a simple, clear way to visually represent information that can be difficult to understand in written form. The five steps below will help you understand and interpret bar graphs. Follow these steps when you answer test questions that include bar graphs.

Steps for Understanding and Interpreting Bar Graphs

STEP 1 Read the title of the bar graph. Read the graph title to determine its topic.

STEP 2 Read the labels. Read the labels for the horizontal axis and the vertical axis.

STEP 3 Read the key that appears on the bar graph. The key indicates what is being represented.

STEP 4 Read the test question about the bar graph. Read through the entire question.

STEP 5 Choose the best answer. Decide which multiple-choice option best fits your answer from Step 4.

Quick Tip
Be sure to read the labels on the graph and the key.

Use the above steps to answer the following questions. Write your answers on a separate sheet of paper.

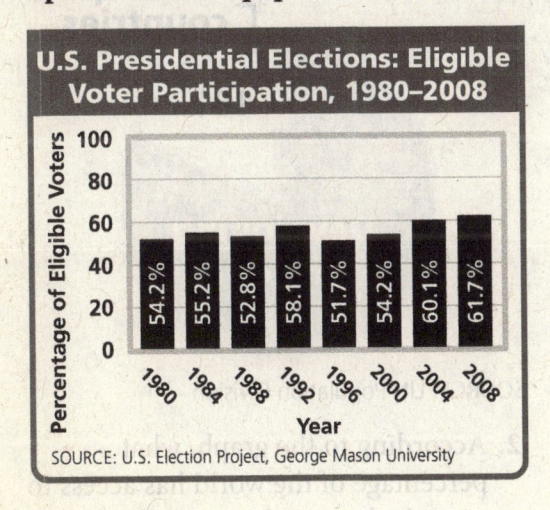

U.S. Presidential Elections: Eligible Voter Participation, 1980–2008

Year	Percentage
1980	54.2%
1984	55.2%
1988	52.8%
1992	58.1%
1996	51.7%
2000	54.2%
2004	60.1%
2008	61.7%

SOURCE: U.S. Election Project, George Mason University

1. What is the title of the graph?
2. What labels are on the horizontal and vertical axis?
3. According to the graph, what percentage of eligible voters participated in the 2000 election?
   A 61.7%
   B 60.1%
   C 54.2%
   D 58.1%

Copyright © Pearson Education, Inc., or its affiliates. All Rights Reserved.

3

Understanding and Interpreting Line and Circle Graphs

Line graphs and circle graphs are simple, clear ways to visually show information. When you break down the process of interpreting graphs into steps, you can analyze the information shown in them and correctly answer test questions.

Steps for Understanding Line and Circle Graphs

STEP 1 Read the title of the graph. The graph title helps you understand the topic.

STEP 2 Identify the key. This information can help you interpret what is shown. Examine the colors, patterns, and shading in the key, and study how they are represented in the graph.

STEP 3 Identify any symbols or labels. Read the labels, and make sure that you understand what each represents.

STEP 4 Identify the graph's main idea. Put the main idea of the graph in your own words.

Quick Tip
Be sure to read the labels on the graph and on the key.

Use the above steps to answer the following questions. Write your answers on a separate sheet of paper.

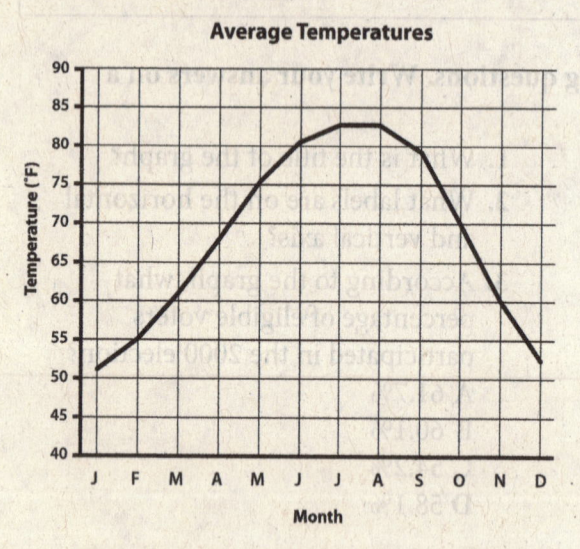

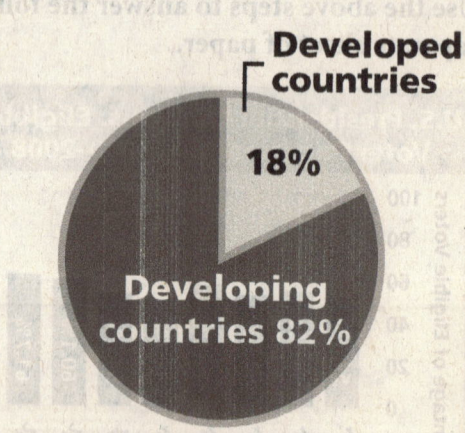

Average Temperatures

World Population, 2008
Developed countries 18%
Developing countries 82%
SOURCE: UN Population Division

1. According to the graph, what is the average yearly temperature in March for this city?
   A 80°F   C 60°F
   B 55°F   D 70°F

2. According to the graph, what percentage of the world has access to a good education?
   A 100%   C 18%
   B 82%   D 28%

Copyright © Pearson Education, Inc., or its affiliates. All Rights Reserved.

Name _____ Class _____ Date _____

Analyzing a Chart or Table

Charts and tables organize large amounts of information into columns and rows. This makes it easier to compare and analyze large amounts of information.

Steps for Analyzing a Chart or Table

STEP 1 Read the title. The title describes the general information included in the chart or table.

STEP 2 Identify the column and subcolumn headings. A column heading is the word or words at the top of each vertical column of information. Sometimes charts and tables have subcolumn headings at different levels.

STEP 3 Read the information in each cell. A row is the information that is presented horizontally in the table. A cell is the intersection of a column and a row.

STEP 4 Determine the relationship among the chart or table entries. Compare and contrast the information.

> **Quick Tip**
> *Rows present information from left to right, and columns present information from top to bottom.*

Using the steps above, evaluate the chart and answer the questions. Write your answers on a separate sheet of paper.

Famous People of the Greek Classical Age		
Person	Famous For	Lived
Aeschylus	Playwright	about 525 B.C. to 456 B.C.
Pericles	Athenian general; made Athens more democratic	495 B.C. to 429 B.C.
Herodotus	Historian	about 484 B.C. to c. 425 B.C.
Socrates	Philosopher	469 B.C. to 399 B.C.
Euripides	Playwright	about 480 B.C. to 406 B.C.
Alexander	King of Macedonia; conqueror of great empire	356 B.C. to 323 B.C.
Thucydides	Historian	about 460 B.C. to about 395 B.C.
Aristophanes	Playwright	about 448 B.C. to 330 B.C.

1. What is the title of this chart?
2. What information is given in each of the columns?
3. What was Alexander famous for?
4. Which famous Greeks were historians?

Copyright © Pearson Education, Inc., or its affiliates. All Rights Reserved.

Analyzing a Map for a Multiple-Choice Question

Multiple-choice questions on a test will sometimes require you to use a map to answer the question. Different parts of the map will help you choose the correct response. Knowing how to read the map will help you find that correct response.

Steps for Analyzing a Map for a Multiple-Choice Question

STEP 1 Identify the map's title, key, scale, and compass rose. The map's title, key, scale, and compass rose help you determine what the map shows.

Quick Tip
Always read the map title first.

STEP 2 Determine what kind of information the map presents. Ask yourself: What is the main type of information on the map?

STEP 3 Read the multiple-choice question. Read through the entire question before choosing an answer.

STEP 4 Decide what part of the map will help you find the answer. Think about the question while looking at the map closely.

STEP 5 Answer the question in your own words without looking at the answer choices. This step will help you locate possible answers.

STEP 6 Eliminate the choices that are obviously wrong. Narrow your list of possible choices further.

STEP 7 Choose the best answer. Choose the best answer that correctly responds to the question.

Use the maps and the steps to answer the following questions. Write your answers on a separate sheet of paper.

1. What does this map show?
   A A man-made lake
   B A mountain range across North Africa
   C A delta created by soil carried by the Nile
   D Political boundaries of countries in North Africa

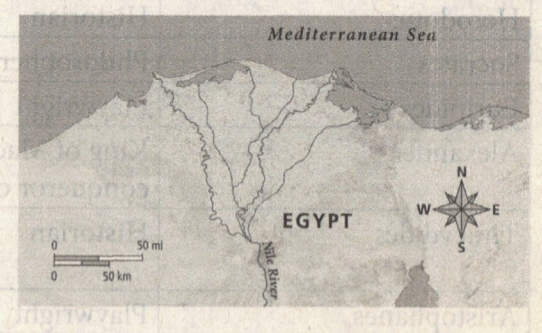

Copyright © Pearson Education, Inc., or its affiliates. All Rights Reserved.

Name _____ Class _____ Date _____

Rubric for Assessing a Report

Grading Criteria	Excellent	Acceptable	Minimal	Unacceptable
Content	Contains many relevant key facts and details; completely and concisely meets requirements; informative graphic organizers.	Contains sufficient facts and details to complete the assignment; includes graphic organizers.	Many necessary facts and details are present; contains some unimportant information.	Important facts and details are missing; much information is irrelevant.
Use of Resources	Uses a range of primary and secondary (six or more); correctly documents organizers.	Uses four appropriate resources; documents sources.	Relies on only one or two sources; sources not documented.	No evidence of resources used.
Organization	Includes interesting introduction; paragraphs logically sequenced and contain subtle transitions; strong conclusion.	Contains introduction; paragraphs are adequately developed but many do not include clear transitions; conclusion is present.	Logical organization; introduction and conclusion not fully developed; transitions between paragraphs missing.	Weak organization; facts and details are stated without connections or transitions; introduction and conclusion inadequate or missing.
Creativity	Demonstrates careful thought and initiative; contains original ideas.	Evidence of some creative thought present.	Contains one or two interesting details.	No original ideas or methods evident.
Presentation	Neatly typed; pages numbered; cover sheet with name, date, and grade; graphics well drawn and attractive.	Easy to read; includes cover sheet and other required features; graphics are neatly presented.	Legible but lacking in visual appeal; missing cover sheet or another required feature; graphics somewhat messy.	Difficult to read; no cover sheet; graphics are illegible.

Copyright © Pearson Education, Inc., or its affiliates. All Rights Reserved.

Name _____ Class _____ Date _____

Rubric for Assessing a Writing Assignment

Grading Criteria	Excellent	Acceptable	Minimal	Unacceptable
Content	Clearly focused introduction; idea development interesting and sophisticated; supporting evidence detailed, accurate, and convincing; perceptive conclusion.	Introduction gives assignment direction; idea development clear; supporting evidence accurate; strong conclusion.	Introduction unclear; idea development uneven and simplistic; supporting evidence uneven; conclusion summarizes information in assignment.	Introduction incomplete, ineffective; idea development ineffective; supporting evidence vague, inaccurate, or missing; conclusion incomplete or missing.
Organization	Paragraph order reinforces content; strong topic sentences make content easy to follow; effective and varied transitions.	Logical paragraph order; clear topic sentences; clear and functional transitions.	Ineffective paragraph order; narrow or inaccurate topic sentences; few clear transitions.	Inconsistent paragraph order; topic sentences and transitions missing.
Mechanics	Flawless punctuation and spelling; varied and interesting sentence structure.	Few spelling and punctuation errors; sentence structure correct.	Some careless spelling and punctuation errors; some errors in sentence structure.	Many spelling and punctuation errors; many sentence fragments and run-ons.

Copyright © Pearson Education, Inc., or its affiliates. All Rights Reserved.

Name _____ Class _____ Date _____

Rubric for Assessing a Student Poster

Grading Criteria	Excellent	Acceptable	Minimal	Unacceptable
Content	Well-written text and carefully chosen visuals work together to illustrate and inform about poster subject.	Descriptive text and appropriate visuals work together to inform viewers.	Text contains inaccuracies, and some visual materials lack pertinence or impact.	Text sparse and inaccurate; visuals lack impact.
Design	Logical and easy to read; type and visuals neatly executed; layout complements the content.	Fairly logical; type and visuals mostly neat and easy to understand.	Somewhat disorganized; fails to complement content.	Disorganized; hastily and carelessly planned.
Visual Appeal	Pleasing use of color, shapes, symbols, and other graphic elements captures viewers' attention and interest.	Good use of color and eye-catching graphic elements.	Good ideas overshadowed by other elements that distract or give a cluttered appearance.	Little constructive use of color or graphic elements.
Creativity	Incorporates unique but pertinent ideas, design elements, visuals, or text that makes the poster stand out.	Contains some unique or imaginative elements.	Contains some good, although not entirely original elements.	No evidence of creativity.

Copyright © Pearson Education, Inc., or its affiliates. All Rights Reserved.

Name _____ Class _____ Date _____

Rubric for Assessing a Letter to the Editor

Grading Criteria	Excellent	Acceptable	Minimal	Unacceptable
Idea Development	Takes a strong, well-defined position; presents appropriate reasons, supporting details, and facts.	Takes a clear position; presents some reasons and details, but does not fully develop argument.	Position not clearly stated; gives unrelated, unsupported general statements, reasons, and details; minimal facts used.	Does not take a clear position; ideas are undeveloped; no facts or details used to support position.
Organization	Contains topic sentence clearly related to position; well-developed paragraphs present ideas and details; transitions are used to enhance organization; strong conclusion evident.	Topic sentence is logical and comprehensive; paragraph order demonstrates clear plan; transitions are clear; conclusion restates position effectively.	Topic sentence blandly states position; paragraphs not ordered effectively; conclusion present but not developed.	No position or conclusion; paragraphs in no particular order; ideas not logically organized.
Mechanics and Style	Sentences interesting and varied; flawless punctuation and spelling; rich vocabulary.	Sentence construction correct and varied; a few punctuation and spelling errors; contains a few rich vocabulary words.	Sentence structure contains some variety, but is incorrect in places; careless errors in spelling and punctuation; weak use of language.	Sentences are repetitious; multiple errors in structure, spelling, and punctuation; weak and incorrect use of vocabulary.
Presentation	Neatly typed; contains date, correct addresses (return and destination), and signature.	Presented neatly, contains necessary elements.	Presented legibly; missing one or two necessary elements.	Difficult to read; lacking important elements, such as signature and return address.

Copyright © Pearson Education, Inc., or its affiliates. All Rights Reserved.

Name _____ Class _____ Date _____

Rubric for Assessing an Oral Presentation

Grading Criteria	Excellent	Acceptable	Minimal	Unacceptable
Preparation	Gathers information from varied sources; makes notecards to use as cues during the presentation; creates attractive visual aids to illustrate the presentation.	Gathers information from three or four sources; prepares notes and visual aids to use during presentation.	Gathers information from one or two sources; writes presentation word-for-word as it will be given.	Gathers information from only one source; may no be able to complete task because of lack of preparation.
Content	Abundance of material clearly related to topic; points clearly made; varied use of materials.	Adequate information about the topic; many good points made; some variation in use of materials.	Some information not connected to the topic.	Information includes little connection to topic.
Organization	Information is well organized and logically ordered; argument easy to follow; conclusion clear.	Most information presented in logical order; argument generally clear and easy to follow.	Ideas loosely connected; organization and flow choppy and somewhat difficult to follow.	No apparent logical order of information in presentation.
Speaking Skills	Enthusiastic, poised, and confident during the presentation; uses complete sentences; speaks clearly.	Engaged during presentation; speaks mostly in complete sentences.	Little or no expression; enunciation not always clear; speaks mostly in sentence fragments.	Appears disinterested during presentation; hard to understand.

Copyright © Pearson Education, Inc., or its affiliates. All Rights Reserved.

Name _____ Class _____ Date _____

Rubric for Assessing a Timeline

Grading Criteria	Excellent	Acceptable	Minimal	Unacceptable
Entry Choice	Great care taken in selection of timeline entries; most significant events, those that show historical patterns, or those that show cause-and-effect relationship selected.	Selections meet assignment criteria; few inaccuracies.	Includes required number of entries; some inaccuracies.	Does not include required number of entries.
Scale and Sequence	Scale consistent and accurate; increments marked; all entries in sequence and placed with care.	Scale accurate; increments marked; entries in sequence.	Scale roughly drawn; increments fairly accurately marked; some entries out of sequence.	No apparent scale; increments not marked; many entries out of sequence.
Mechanics	Flawless.	Few mechanical errors.	Some errors in spelling and dates.	Many errors in spelling and dates.
Visual Presentation	Visually striking; very effective in communicating historical information.	Clear and uncluttered.	Legible.	Illegible and messy.

Copyright © Pearson Education, Inc., or its affiliates. All Rights Reserved.

Name _____ Class _____ Date _____

Core Concepts Part 1
Tools of Geography

Test A

Key Terms
Complete each statement.

1. Map makers use units called _____ to measure latitude and longitude on Earth's surface.

2. Geographers use the term _____ to describe one half of Earth.

3. Images such as _____ can show certain features in greater detail than maps can.

4. Modern geographers sometimes use _____, which are computer devices that store data about locations.

5. Map makers use different types of _____ to show flat images of Earth's rounded surface.

6. Some maps include a _____ to show the broader location of the area displayed on the main map.

7. The _____ on a map shows the major directions for the area displayed on that map.

8. To find out how many U.S. states border Mexico, you would look at a _____.

9. If you say that Canada is north of the United States, you are giving a _____ for each country.

10. Geographers would define an area that shared a common climate as a single _____ in terms of its weather.

Key Ideas
Identify the choice that best completes the statement or answers the question.

____ 11. Most maps have a key and a scale bar in order to
   a. display degrees of longitude and latitude.
   b. indicate north, south, east, and west.
   c. provide information on distance and map symbols.
   d. show the area on the map in relationship to a larger area.

____ 12. What type of map would you use to find the elevation of mountain ranges?
   a. A physical map
   b. A political map
   c. A special-purpose map
   d. A road map

____ 13. Which of the following is one of the five themes of geography that is useful when studying different places?
   a. Political history
   b. Economics
   c. Culture
   d. Movement

Copyright © Pearson Education, Inc., or its affiliates. All Rights Reserved.

Name _____ Class _____ Date _____

Core Concepts Part 1
Tools of Geography

Test A

Critical Thinking

14. Why would you use a map instead of a globe or an aerial photograph to find your way around a city?

_____
_____
_____

15. How would you find the distance, in miles, between two points on a map?

_____
_____
_____

16. Describe the major physical and human features of the location where you live, such as the landscape, weather, and population. What theme of geography are you using in your description?

_____
_____
_____

Essay

17. NASA wants to show the surface of the planet Mars using the same tools that geographers use to show Earth's surface. Apply your knowledge of the available types of tools and maps to describe what general kinds of Mars data they would display.

_____
_____
_____
_____
_____
_____
_____
_____
_____

Name _____ Class _____ Date _____

Core Concepts Part 1
Tools of Geography

Test B

Key Terms

Complete each statement.

1. Lines of _____ measure the distance north or south of the Equator.

2. North-south lines on a globe measure _____, the distance east or west of the Prime Meridian.

3. Showing our round Earth on a flat surface leads to _____ in the shape or position of objects.

4. Modern geographers can view _____, pictures of Earth's surface taken from orbit.

5. Look at the _____ of a map to understand the meaning of that map's symbols and shading.

6. To find out how much real-world distance is represented by a given space on a map, look at the _____ of that map.

7. By looking at a _____, geographers can quickly locate and identify natural features of an area.

8. Areas of low _____ are often found close to the seashore.

9. The _____ of the Capitol Building is 38°54'N, 77°2'W.

10. The geographic theme of _____ deals with how people, goods, and ideas travel from one place to another.

Key Ideas

Identify the choice that best completes the statement or answers the question.

____ 11. Which part of a map would you look at to find directions on a physical map?
   a. Scale bar
   b. Compass rose
   c. Locator map
   d. Key

____ 12. What type of map would you look at to find the voting results for a recent presidential election?
   a. A political map
   b. A physical map
   c. A special-purpose map
   d. A Mercator projection map

____ 13. When a geographer studies the migration patterns of humans over many centuries and how that has affected the geography of North America, which theme of geography is he or she using?
   a. Location
   b. Region
   c. Place
   d. Movement

Copyright © Pearson Education, Inc., or its affiliates. All Rights Reserved.

Name _____ Class _____ Date _____

Core Concepts Part 1
Tools of Geography

Test B

Critical Thinking

14. What advantages does a globe have over a map or a satellite image?

_____
_____
_____

15. Explain why a compass rose appears on many different types of maps.

_____
_____
_____

16. Describe the location of your school in relation to a nearby building. What theme of geography are you using?

_____
_____
_____

Essay

17. You have been asked to send visual information about your hometown to students in a foreign country. Describe the different geographic tools and types of maps that you could use to show your hometown. Then, choose one type of map and one other method that would best display geographic information about your community. Support your selections.

_____
_____
_____
_____
_____
_____
_____
_____
_____
_____

Copyright © Pearson Education, Inc., or its affiliates. All Rights Reserved.

Name _____ Class _____ Date _____

Core Concepts Part 2
Our Planet Earth

Test A

Key Terms

Complete each statement.

1. Earth travels around the Sun along an oval-shaped path called an _____.

2. During an _____, days and nights are nearly equal in length.

3. The world is divided into many areas that share the same time, known as _____.

4. The continents and the ocean floor are both part of Earth's _____.

5. Water, ice, and wind are some of the forces that cause the _____ of rock and soil.

6. A flat area rising above the surrounding land is called a _____.

7. Earth's crust is made of huge _____ that move very slowly.

Key Ideas

Identify the choice that best completes the statement or answers the question.

____ 8. Day and night are caused by
   a. the rotation of Earth on its axis.
   b. the revolution of Earth around the sun.
   c. the orbit of the Moon around Earth.
   d. the distance from Earth to the sun.

____ 9. If it is noon in New York, which is Eastern Standard Time, what time is it in Denver, which is Mountain Standard Time?
   a. 2 P.M.
   b. 11 A.M.
   c. 10 A.M.
   d. 9 A.M.

____ 10. What causes volcanoes to erupt?
   a. The movement of continental plates creates pressure that pushes magma to Earth's surface.
   b. Continental plates rub against each other and cause vibrations in Earth's core.
   c. Moving continental plates push against each other and raise up Earth's crust.
   d. Pressure builds up at seams in Earth's crust, causing it to shake and release magma.

____ 11. One of the many ways that the process of deposition contributes to changing Earth's surface includes
   a. breaking down large landforms such as a plateaus.
   b. fracturing rocks when water freezes.
   c. building up a mountain range.
   d. creating beaches along the coastline.

Core Concepts

Copyright © Pearson Education, Inc., or its affiliates. All Rights Reserved.

Core Concepts Part 2
Our Planet Earth

Test A

Critical Thinking

12. How does the tilt of Earth's axis and its movement around the sun play a part in the changing of the seasons in the northern hemisphere?

13. What role does the mantle play in shaping Earth's crust?

14. Which landforms described in this lesson are formed by processes of deposition?

Essay

15. Describe the movements of the seven continents. Analyze this movement and hypothesize how the world's landmasses may look different in the future if the continents continue to move. What events might occur where continental plates push together?

Name _____ Class _____ Date _____

Core Concepts Part 2
Our Planet Earth

Test B

Key Terms

Complete each statement.

1. Earth rotates along its _____, an imaginary line drawn between the North and South Poles.

2. The _____ is a period during which days are longest in one hemisphere and shortest in the other.

3. The Earth's inner _____ is made of solid metal.

4. Shapes or kinds of land are called _____.

5. The process called _____ breaks rocks down into much smaller pieces.

6. The process of _____ can slowly create new landforms by piling up sand or small rocks.

7. The theory of _____ helps explain the movement of Earth's continents.

Key Ideas

Identify the choice that best completes the statement or answers the question.

____ 8. Time in the region surrounding the Prime Meridian is sometimes called
   a. Prime Time.
   b. London Mean Time.
   c. Global Standard Time.
   d. Universal Time.

____ 9. When it is daytime in New York City,
   a. it is daytime in the eastern hemisphere.
   b. it is nighttime on the opposite side of Earth.
   c. it is daytime across the United States.
   d. it is nighttime in the southern hemisphere.

____ 10. What causes earthquakes?
   a. Plates slide against one another, often at faults.
   b. Pressure builds up in the molten rock beneath Earth's crust and causes it to shake.
   c. Continental plates pull apart from each other, causing the crust to collapse.
   d. Continental plates press together and suddenly push up the crust.

____ 11. Weathering and erosion impact human settlement patterns because as these processes break down landforms and rocks into smaller pieces, they also contribute to
   a. dividing the continent into watersheds.
   b. generating volcanoes.
   c. creating beaches along the coastlines.
   d. providing soil for agriculture.

Copyright © Pearson Education, Inc., or its affiliates. All Rights Reserved.

Name _____ Class _____ Date _____

Core Concepts Part 2
Our Planet Earth

Test B

Critical Thinking

12. Why do the northern and southern hemispheres experience different seasons in the months of June and December?

_____
_____
_____

13. What problems would life on Earth face if the planet had no atmosphere?

_____
_____
_____

14. What landforms discussed in this lesson are shaped or formed by the process of erosion? Give an example of how one landform is shaped by this process.

_____
_____
_____
_____

Essay

15. Contrast the processes acting above the Earth's surface that build up landforms with the processes acting below the Earth's surface that also build up landforms. How do these two sets of processes compare to those that wear down Earth's landforms?

_____
_____
_____
_____
_____
_____
_____
_____
_____
_____

Copyright © Pearson Education, Inc., or its affiliates. All Rights Reserved.

Name _____ Class _____ Date _____

Core Concepts Part 3
Climates and Ecosystems

Test A

Key Terms
Complete each statement.

1. The area between the Tropic of Cancer and the Arctic Circle is one of Earth's two _____.

3. By looking outside to decide what you will wear that day, you are checking the _____.

4. The three parts of the water cycle are _____, condensation, and precipitation.

5. A _____ is type of tropical cyclone that forms over the Atlantic Ocean.

6. A _____ is a park-like landscape of grasslands with scattered trees that can survive dry spells.

7. Maritime climates exist where moist winds blow _____.

Key Ideas
Identify the choice that best completes the statement or answers the question.

_____ 7. What is the primary reason that some areas of Earth are consistently warmer than other areas of Earth?
   a. Distance from the sun
   b. Tilt of Earth's axis
   c. Altitude
   d. Seasons

_____ 8. _____ act like large rivers in the Earth's oceans and help spread Earth's heat and shape climates.
   a. Ocean currents
   b. Wind patterns
   c. Temperature differences
   d. Water cycles

_____ 9. When two air masses of different temperatures or moisture content collide, one result of this air movement may be
   a. high pressure.
   b. low pressure.
   c. a new desert area.
   d. intense storms.

_____ 10. Ecosystems can change over time because of physical processes or
   a. grass or forest fires.
   b. hurricanes or tornadoes.
   c. very cold winters.
   d. human activities.

Copyright © Pearson Education, Inc., or its affiliates. All Rights Reserved.

Name _____ Class _____ Date _____

Core Concepts Part 3
Climates and Ecosystems

Test A

Critical Thinking

11. What causes temperatures in the high latitudes to be cool in the summer and bitterly cold in the winter?

_____
_____
_____

12. How does a belt of rising and sinking air form?

_____
_____
_____

13. Discuss how temperature, precipitation, and wind interact to form arid climates.

_____
_____
_____
_____

Essay

14. Discuss the relationship between temperature, wind, and air currents, and how each affects climate types. Give examples.

_____
_____
_____
_____
_____
_____
_____
_____
_____
_____
_____
_____
_____

Copyright © Pearson Education, Inc., or its affiliates. All Rights Reserved.

Name _____ Class _____ Date _____

Core Concepts Part 3
Climates and Ecosystems

Test B

Key Terms
Complete each statement.

1. By measuring the average day-to-day weather of a place over many years, you can describe the _____ of that place.

2. Heat from sunlight can cause water to _____ from a body of water on Earth.

3. The area of rising air near the equator is called the _____.

4. Hurricanes affect larger areas than _____, which are swirling funnels of wind.

5. The difference between deciduous trees and coniferous trees is that coniferous trees do not _____.

6. The climate types found where there is steadily sinking air are _____.

Key Ideas
Identify the choice that best completes the statement or answers the question.

____ 7. What causes some areas of Earth to be warmer than other areas?
   a. Distance from the sun
   b. Tilt of Earth's axis
   c. Altitude
   d. Seasons

____ 8. The two main ways to describe both weather and climate are _____ and temperature.
   a. wind speed
   b. precipitation
   c. weather pattern
   d. climate graph

____ 9. The Canary Current and the Labrador Current move cool water from the poles to the tropics, where the cool water _____ the air near it.
   a. chills
   b. warms
   c. condenses
   d. clouds

____ 10. _____, which move heat and moisture between different parts of the Earth, may lead to cyclones, hurricanes, and tornadoes.
   a. Convergence zones
   b. Wind and air currents
   c. Bands of rising air
   d. Bands of sinking air

Copyright © Pearson Education, Inc., or its affiliates. All Rights Reserved.

Name _____ Class _____ Date _____

Core Concepts Part 3
Climates and Ecosystems

Test B

Critical Thinking

11. What are the three zones of latitude and why are some zones warmer than others?

_____
_____
_____
_____

12. What happens when warm air rises and loses its moisture? What effect does that have on the regions at edges of the tropics and near the poles?

_____
_____
_____
_____
_____

13. Which of the three shapers of climate—temperature, precipitation, and wind—do you think is most important in the formation of arid climates?

_____
_____
_____
_____
_____

Essay

14. Explain how temperature, wind, and water are important to the water cycle.

_____
_____
_____
_____
_____
_____
_____
_____
_____
_____
_____
_____
_____

Copyright © Pearson Education, Inc., or its affiliates. All Rights Reserved.

Name _____ Class _____ Date _____

Core Concepts Part 4
Human-Environment Interaction

Test A

Key Terms

Complete each statement.

1. When _____ resources are used up, they are gone for good, because they cannot be replenished.

2. The ways people use land are affected by both the _____ and their culture.

3. Land uses that cover large areas include cropland, forests, and _____.

4. Animals that live in a forest may be harmed if people bring about the _____ of a region.

Key ideas

Identify the choice that best completes the statement or answers the question.

____ 5. A useful material found in the environment is known as a
   a. nonrenewable resource.
   b. energy resource.
   c. natural resource.
   d. renewable resource.

____ 6. Which of the following is an example of a nonrenewable resource?
   a. Oil
   b. Soil
   c. Water
   d. Animals

____ 7. _____ is the movement of new settlers and their culture into a new area.
   a. Land use
   b. Colonization
   c. Industrialization
   d. Environmental change

____ 8. Both deforestation and drilling oil wells can reduce
   a. ecosystems.
   b. biodiversity.
   c. pollution.
   d. spillover.

____ 9. Pollution is considered a spillover because
   a. it is often caused by chemical spills.
   b. the environment can't absorb enough of the pollutants.
   c. water pollution is the most dangerous type of pollution.
   d. it affects parts of the environment not involved in the activity that caused the pollution.

Copyright © Pearson Education, Inc., or its affiliates. All Rights Reserved.

Name _____ Class _____ Date _____

Core Concepts Part 4
Human-Environment Interaction

Test A

Critical Thinking

10. Discuss the impact that colonization may have on land use.

_____
_____
_____
_____

11. Where in the United States would you most likely find much of the nation's agricultural activities?

_____
_____
_____
_____

12. What does it mean that people extract natural resources from the environment? How can extracting resources harm ecosystems and the environment?

_____
_____
_____
_____

Essay

13. How might colonization and industrialization affect renewable and nonrenewable resources?

_____
_____
_____
_____
_____
_____
_____
_____
_____
_____

Name _____ Class _____ Date _____

Core Concepts Part 4
Human-Environment Interaction

Test B

Key Terms

Complete each statement.

1. Humans depend on their _____ to provide food, water, energy, and other materials that are necessary for human survival.

2. Soil, plants, water, and animals are all examples of major _____ resources.

3. Technology has made it possible for people to change their environment by building _____ on the edges of cities and large towns.

4. When pollution affects someone or something not involved in the activity that produces the pollution, this effect is called a _____.

Key Ideas

Identify the choice that best completes the statement or answers the question.

____ 5. It is unlikely that Earth will ever run out of
   a. petroleum.
   b. plants.
   c. minerals.
   d. natural gas.

____ 6. Since the 1800s, what human activity has changed landscapes and led to the growth of large cities in many countries?
   a. Industrialization
   b. Colonization
   c. Suburbs
   d. Technology

____ 7. Which factor is most likely to change a region's landscape?
   a. Temperature
   b. Climate
   c. Oceans
   d. Settlers

____ 8. Some chemicals used by farmers may harm the environment by causing
   a. deforestation.
   b. oil spills.
   c. pollution.
   d. spillover.

____ 9. A common reason for pollution is that it is produced by an activity that
   a. should never be done.
   b. has no beneficial impacts.
   c. is against the law.
   d. leads to economic growth.

Copyright © Pearson Education, Inc., or its affiliates. All Rights Reserved.

Name _____ Class _____ Date _____

Core Concepts Part 4
Human-Environment Interaction

Test B

Critical Thinking

10. How have industrialization and the growth of cities changed land use in some areas of the United States?
_____
_____
_____

11. What determines the way in which people use land? What are some things that can change the way in which land is used?
_____
_____
_____
_____

12. How can using resources for growing food or producing other goods and services affect the environment?
_____
_____
_____
_____

Essay

13. What is biodiversity? Do you think that biodiversity is important? Why or why not?
_____
_____
_____
_____
_____
_____
_____
_____
_____
_____

Name _____ Class _____ Date _____

Core Concepts Part 5
Economics and Geography

Test A

Key Terms

Complete each statement.

1. A(n) _____ is a factor that encourages people to make choices to act in a certain way.

2. _____ is the desire for a certain good or service.

3. _____ is the money a company has left after subtracting the costs of doing business.

4. A general increase in prices over time is called _____.

5. An economy in which the central government makes all economic decisions is a(n) _____.

6. A(n) _____ is a country with a strong economy and a high standard of living.

7. The amount of goods and services produced given the amount of resources used is called _____.

8. _____ are goods and services produced within a country and sold outside the country's borders.

9. A government policy or restriction that limits international trade is a(n) _____.

10. The price paid for borrowing money is _____.

11. A(n) _____ is a share of ownership in a company.

Key Ideas

Identify the choice that best completes the statement or answers the question.

____ 12. Which type of economic system has the highest level of government control?
   a. Traditional economy
   b. Market economy
   c. Command economy
   d. Mixed economy

____ 13. Which of the following are ways to increase economic development?
   a. Encouraging more farming
   b. Investing in education and training
   c. Establishing price controls
   d. Lowering wages

____ 14. Which describes the type of buying and selling that takes place within a country?
   a. Free trade
   b. International trade
   c. Tariff
   d. Domestic trade

Copyright © Pearson Education, Inc., or its affiliates. All Rights Reserved.

Name _____ Class _____ Date _____

Core Concepts Part 5
Economics and Geography

Test A

Critical Thinking

15. What happens to producers and consumers during a recession?

_____
_____
_____

16. What is the role of the government in a mixed economy?

_____
_____
_____

17. How can technology affect a country's economic development?

_____
_____
_____

Essay

18. Would people in a developed country or a developing country be more likely to invest their money? How does that affect the people's well-being?

_____
_____
_____
_____
_____
_____
_____
_____
_____
_____

Name _____ Class _____ Date _____

Core Concepts Part 5
Economics and Geography

Test B

Key Terms
Complete each statement.

1. The amount of a good that is available for use is known as _____.

2. A(n) _____ is an organized way for producers and consumers to trade goods and services.

3. The act of concentrating on a limited number of goods or activities is known as _____.

4. Companies' profits are affected by _____, which is the struggle among producers for consumers' money.

5. A(n) _____ is an economy in which individual consumers and producers make economic decisions.

6. _____ is economic growth, or an increase in living standards.

7. _____ is the practical application of knowledge to accomplish a task.

8. _____ are goods and services sold in a country that are produced in other countries.

9. Today, many countries are working toward _____, or the removal of trade barriers.

10. _____ is an arrangement in which a buyer can borrow money to purchase something and pay for it over time.

11. _____ is the act of using money to try to make a future profit.

Key Ideas
Identify the choice that best completes the statement or answers the question.

____ 12. Most societies have which type of economic system?
   a. Traditional economy
   b. Market economy
   c. Command economy
   d. Mixed economy

____ 13. Compared to a developing country, a developed country is likely to have which of the following?
   a. A less-productive economy
   b. Lower standards of living
   c. A stronger economy
   d. Lower productivity

____ 14. Which of the following is a likely result of trade barriers?
   a. Protection of domestic producers from competition
   b. Lower prices
   c. More choices
   d. Increase in imports

Copyright © Pearson Education, Inc., or its affiliates. All Rights Reserved.

Name _____ Class _____ Date _____

Core Concepts Part 5
Economics and Geography

Test B

Critical Thinking

15. How can a recession lead to unemployment?

_____
_____
_____

16. What is one similarity and one difference between the economies of Japan and Cuba?

_____
_____
_____

17. How can improving education and training for a country's people affect the country's development?

_____
_____
_____

Essay

18. What are some characteristics of a country that may influence its leaders to prefer tariffs? What are some characteristics that may cause a country's leaders to prefer free trade?

_____
_____
_____
_____
_____
_____
_____
_____
_____
_____

Copyright © Pearson Education, Inc., or its affiliates. All Rights Reserved.

Name _____ Class _____ Date _____

Core Concepts Part 6
Population and Movement

Test A

Key Terms
Complete each statement.

1. The _____ is the number of live births per 1,000 people in a year.

2. The number of people per square mile or other unit of land area is known as the _____ of that area.

3. Migration may be described as _____ migration, emigration, or immigration.

4. _____ attract people to new countries.

5. People in poor, overcrowded neighborhoods, called _____, often live in shacks or run-down buildings.

6. The movement of people from rural areas to urban areas is called _____.

7. In _____ sprawl, new, spread-out neighborhoods replace farmland and wilderness areas.

Key Ideas
Identify the choice that best completes the statement or answers the question.

____ 8. A country's _____ is the total number of people living within its borders.
   a. population density
   b. population
   c. population growth
   d. population distribution

____ 9. Causes of migration that push people to leave their home country are called
   a. pull factors.
   b. push factors.
   c. new customs.
   d. involuntary migrations.

____ 10. _____ and _____ are two problems created by urbanization.
   a. More jobs; new highways
   b. Slums; suburban sprawl
   c. Education; better lives for children
   d. Better health care; new water lines

____ 11. One cause for the rapid population growth since the time of the Industrial Revolution is
   a. better medical care.
   b. high infant mortality.
   c. food shortages.
   d. poor sanitation.

Copyright © Pearson Education, Inc., or its affiliates. All Rights Reserved.

Name _____ Class _____ Date _____

Core Concepts Part 6
Population and Movement

Test A

Critical Thinking

12. How can rapid population growth affect the infant mortality rate?
_____
_____
_____
_____

13. What are two reasons that people from all over the world emigrate to the United States?
_____
_____
_____
_____

14. What is urbanization, and how does it affect people who are long-time city residents?
_____
_____
_____
_____
_____

Essay

15. How can demographers use a country's population distribution and population density to help governments prepare for the future?
_____
_____
_____
_____
_____
_____
_____
_____
_____
_____
_____
_____

Name _____ Class _____ Date _____

Core Concepts Part 6
Population and Movement

Test B

Key Terms
Complete each statement.

1. The _____ is the number of deaths per 1,000 people in a year.

2. Unfortunately, problems caused by rapid population growth can lead to deaths of many infants, giving an area a high _____.

3. How people are spread out over an area of land is that area's _____.

4. A newcomer who arrives from elsewhere and settles in a new country is called a(n) _____.

5. Cities with high population densities tend to have crowded roads and crowded _____.

6. _____ migrations have generally involved the forced movement of enslaved people.

7. One of the challenges of urban growth is suburban _____.

Key Ideas
Identify the choice that best completes the statement or answers the question.

____ 8. A tool used to describe how thickly or thinly an area is settled is called
   a. population density.
   b. total population.
   c. population growth.
   d. population distribution.

____ 9. A _____ is one example of a pull factor.
   a. flood
   b. famine
   c. war
   d. supply of good jobs

____ 10. People who live in poor, overcrowded urban areas, or _____, are unable to meet their basic needs.
   a. urban areas
   b. slums
   c. rural areas
   d. suburbs

____ 11. Rapid population growth can result in large increases in the infant morality rate if there is
   a. a shortage of food and clean water.
   b. a higher consumption of goods and services.
   c. an industrial plant located nearby.
   d. an extended period of migration.

Copyright © Pearson Education, Inc., or its affiliates. All Rights Reserved.

Name _____ Class _____ Date _____

Core Concepts Part 6
Population and Movement

Test B

Critical Thinking

12. How can population growth affect the environment?

_____
_____
_____

13. How is it possible for the total population of a country to grow even when the country's population growth rate is very small?

_____
_____
_____

14. How might spreading suburbs affect the lives of the people who are living on the farmland and in the open spaces?

_____
_____
_____

Essay

15. How can migration change a country's plans for population growth, distribution, and density? What impact can migration have on planning?

_____
_____
_____
_____
_____
_____
_____
_____
_____
_____

Name _____ Class _____ Date _____

Core Concepts Part 7
Culture and Geography

Test A

Key Terms
Complete each statement.

1. Human activities create geographic areas that have been shaped by people, which are also called _____.

2. A pattern of organized relationships among groups of people within a society is a(n) _____.

3. A family that includes parents, children, grandparents, aunts, uncles, and other family members is a(n) _____ family.

4. People who speak different languages sometimes turn to a(n) _____ in order to communicate with each other.

5. Religion can help guide people in standards of acceptable behavior, or _____.

6. Settlement, trade, migration, and communication are among the ways that _____ takes place.

Key Ideas
Identify the choice that best completes the statement or answers the question.

____ 7. A group of humans with a shared culture who have organized themselves to meet their basic needs is a(n)
   a. family.
   b. society.
   c. social structure.
   d. extended family.

____ 8. In a society, architectural works can be important _____ symbols.
   a. government
   b. cultural
   c. geographical
   d. resource

____ 9. Cultures often develop along with science and
   a. tools.
   b. technology.
   c. agriculture.
   d. machines.

____ 10. An area in which a single culture or cultural trait is dominant is called a
   a. culture.
   b. cultural landscape.
   c. norm.
   d. culture region.

Copyright © Pearson Education, Inc., or its affiliates. All Rights Reserved.

Name _____ Class _____ Date _____

Core Concepts Part 7
Culture and Geography

Test A

Critical Thinking

11. Do political boundaries always match the boundaries of culture regions? Explain your reasoning.

_____
_____
_____
_____

12. How do cultures change?

_____
_____
_____
_____

13. Why was refrigeration such an important technological development?

_____
_____
_____
_____

Essay

14. Do you think that some cultures change faster than others? Why or why not? Explain your reasoning.

_____
_____
_____
_____
_____
_____
_____
_____
_____
_____

Name _____ Class _____ Date _____

Core Concepts Part 7
Culture and Geography

Test B

Key Terms
Complete each statement.

1. A behavior that is considered normal in a particular society is a(n) _____.

2. A(n) _____ family is one consisting of parents and their children.

3. The world has about 12 major language groups. Languages within each of these groups share a common _____.

4. Ramadan, a time to avoid food during daytime, to pray, and to read the Quran, is a holy month for _____.

5. The thousands of distinct religious traditions that tend to be passed down by word of mouth instead of through sacred text are called _____.

6. When customs and ideas are spread by settlement, trade, migration, and communication from one culture to another, _____ is taking place.

Key Ideas
Identify the choice that best completes the statement or answers the question.

____ 7. Industrial societies often organize members according to their
   a. social structure.
   b. families.
   c. agriculture.
   d. social class.

____ 8. Love, death, peace, and war are examples of _____ that relate to the entire world.
   a. paintings
   b. music
   c. books
   d. universal themes

____ 9. Some people worry that rapid communication is creating a new global culture that threatens
   a. migration.
   b. cultural hearths.
   c. diversity.
   d. communication.

____ 10. The basis for culture is
   a. language.
   b. sounds.
   c. symbols.
   d. gestures.

Copyright © Pearson Education, Inc., or its affiliates. All Rights Reserved.

Name _____ Class _____ Date _____

Core Concepts Part 7
Culture and Geography

Test B

Critical Thinking

11. Why are parts of southwest Asia and northern Africa joined in a single culture region?

_____

_____

_____

12. What do you think is the reason that it usually takes time for a culture to change?

_____

_____

_____

13. How is a Sumerian chariot from about 5,000 years ago different from a convertible automobile from the 1950s? How are the two vehicles similar?

_____

_____

_____

_____

Essay

14. Why are language and religion so important to culture and society?

_____

_____

_____

_____

_____

_____

_____

_____

_____

_____

_____

_____

Copyright © Pearson Education, Inc., or its affiliates. All Rights Reserved.

Name _____ Class _____ Date _____

Core Concepts Part 8
Government and Citizenship

Test A

Key Terms

Complete each statement.

1. Most modern governments have a(n) _____ that outlines the rules and principles of their organization.

2. The leaders of the government have the power to make all decisions for the country in a(n) _____ government.

3. All laws are passed by the central government under a(n) _____.

4. Countries create _____ to describe how they plan to interact with the governments of other countries.

5. If two or more countries have a conflict, they may sign a(n) _____ to help resolve it.

6. Voting is one example of taking part in government, also called _____.

Key Ideas

Identify the choice that best completes the statement or answers the question.

____ 7. A state containing several countries is called
   a. an empire.
   b. a monarchy.
   c. a democracy.
   d. communist.

____ 8. The principle of majority rule means that the U.S. government
   a. can pass any law without worrying about minority rights.
   b. can only pass laws voted for by a majority of representatives.
   c. is bound by the rule of law.
   d. must have the support of a majority of local governments for the action of the regional government.

____ 9. Which of the following statements is most accurate?
   a. In the past, there were many democracies that protected the rights of citizens.
   b. The rise of democracies that protect citizens' rights is a fairly recent event in world history.
   c. There are very few democratic governments in the world today.
   d. Most democracies fail to protect the rights of their citizens.

____ 10. Which of the following is an example of something that a limited government would do, but is probably something that an unlimited government would not be willing to do?
   a. Build and maintain public roads
   b. Protect citizens from attack
   c. Operate public schools
   d. Let citizens speak freely in public

Name _____ Class _____ Date _____

Core Concepts Part 8
Government and Citizenship

Test A

Critical Thinking

11. Compare and contrast the governments of ancient Athens and the United States.

12. Compare the legislative, executive, and judicial branches of the U.S. government. Consider the highest office or institution in each branch; the role of each branch in making, enforcing, or interpreting laws; and any other powers each branch has. Compare and contrast the governments of ancient Athens and the United States.

13. What role does the United Nations play in global diplomacy and human rights?

Essay

14. Why might a nation cooperate with some countries and come into conflict with others? Do you think that the types of governments that two countries have can make them more or less likely to cooperate with each other? Explain.

Copyright © Pearson Education, Inc., or its affiliates. All Rights Reserved.

Name _____ Class _____ Date _____

Core Concepts Part 8
Government and Citizenship

Test B

Key Terms

Complete each statement.

1. Laws restrict the powers of a(n) _____ government.

2. The unjust use of power is known as _____.

3. The United States has a(n) _____, in which power is divided between different levels of government.

4. Most governments use _____ to manage their relationships with each other in a peaceful way.

5. _____ includes all those activities that have to do with a person's society and community.

6. Members of a(n) _____ try to influence public policy on specific issues.

Key Ideas

Identify the choice that best completes the statement or answers the question.

____ 7. Which form of government has a king or queen that shares powers with the people of the state and the other branches of government?
   a. Absolute monarchy
   b. Constitutional monarchy
   c. Representative democracy
   d. Authoritarian communism

____ 8. The principle of giving each branch of government the power to cancel the action of another branch is called
   a. separation of powers.
   b. checks and balances.
   c. the federal system.
   d. minority rights.

____ 9. Which of the following statements best describes human rights in the world today?
   a. All people around the world are part of a global community, so everyone enjoys the same rights.
   b. Democracies are most likely to protect human rights of their citizens.
   c. There is less support for human rights around the world today than there was in the past.
   d. Non-democratic governments usually protect the basic rights of their citizens

____ 10. Which of the following international organizations works to prevent and solve economic crises around the world?
   a. United Nations
   b. Amnesty International
   c. World Bank
   d. International Monetary Fund

Copyright © Pearson Education, Inc., or its affiliates. All Rights Reserved.

Name _____ Class _____ Date _____

Core Concepts Part 8
Government and Citizenship

Test B

Critical Thinking

11. Compare and contrast limited and unlimited governments.

_____
_____
_____
_____

12. Compare and contrast states and nation-states.

_____
_____
_____
_____
_____

13. In what ways do governments and international organizations try to address the harmful effects of conflict?

_____
_____
_____
_____

Essay

14. Would you have the same rights and responsibilities if you were a citizen of another country? What are the sorts of things that might contribute to your rights being the same or different in another country?

_____
_____
_____
_____
_____
_____
_____
_____
_____
_____

Copyright © Pearson Education, Inc., or its affiliates. All Rights Reserved.

Name _____ Class _____ Date _____

Core Concepts Part 9
Tools of History

Test A

Key Terms
Complete each statement.

1. A _____ is a line marked off with a series of events and dates.
2. The time before humans invented writing is called _____.
3. A(n) _____ is information that comes directly from a person who experienced an event.
4. An encyclopedia article describing a historical event that took place 250 years ago is an example of a _____ source.
5. The study of humankind in all aspects, especially development and culture, is _____.
6. A person who explores places where people once lived, searching for artifacts to learn about the past, is practicing _____.
7. A(n) _____ would be a good source to use if you wanted to understand how landforms like rivers and hills affected a battle.

Key Ideas
Identify the choice that best completes the statement or answers the question.

_____ 8. Which of the following is a list of events, organized in the order in which they occurred?
   a. Period
   b. Chronology
   c. Era
   d. Epoch

_____ 9. What type of information can be shown best on a historical map?
   a. Migration
   b. Weather
   c. Political boundaries
   d. Population

_____ 10. What element of a historical map is most likely to tell you what period of time the map shows?
   a. Locator map
   b. Key
   c. Title
   d. Shape

_____ 11. Which of the following is true for historians evaluating the reliability of primary sources?
   a. Because the source witnessed the events, a historian can trust it completely.
   b. Only sources provided by college professors are considered reliable.
   c. Sources must be compared to articles from the Internet.
   d. A historian must look for evidence of bias.

Core Concepts Part 9
Tools of History

Test A

Critical Thinking

12. Which of these types of primary sources—letters, diary entries, speeches, artifacts—would be least likely to show bias? Explain your answer.

_____
_____
_____

13. Why do historians study primary sources?

_____
_____
_____
_____

14. Why might some ancient cultures have had strong oral traditions?

_____
_____
_____
_____

Essay

15. If you wanted to research a topic in history, would a primary source or a secondary source be more valuable? Explain your answer.

_____
_____
_____
_____
_____
_____
_____
_____
_____
_____
_____

Name _____ Class _____ Date _____

Core Concepts Part 9
Tools of History

Test B

Key Terms
Complete each statement.

1. A person who studies events that took place during the past is a _____.

2. A list of events in the order in which they occurred is called a _____.

3. A(n) _____ is information about an event that does not come from a person who experienced that event.

4. An example of a _____ source is photograph taken on the day of a historic event.

5. A(n) _____ is an unfair preference for or dislike of something or someone.

6. The scientific study of ancient cultures through the examination of artifacts and other evidence is called _____.

7. Someone who studies _____ seeks to understand the origin of humans and how humans developed physically.

Key Ideas
Identify the choice that best completes the statement or answers the question.

____ 8. A song about a hunt may form an important part of a society's
   a. artifacts.
   b. archaeology.
   c. anthropology.
   d. oral tradition.

____ 9. Why is a historical map a good type of map to use to study trade patterns?
   a. A historical map shows place names.
   b. A historical map can show movement over time.
   c. A historical map has a compass rose.
   d. A historical map has a key.

____ 10. What type of information do historical maps offer?
   a. Primary
   b. Archaeological
   c. Oral
   d. Visual

____ 11. Which of the following is a reason why historians may want to consider a source's opinions as well as the facts reported by a source?
   a. A source that a historian trusts is likely to have true opinions.
   b. The opinions may provide clues to the source's feelings and possible bias.
   c. Examining opinions will reveal whether it is a primary or secondary source.
   d. The opinions will reveal the identity of the source.

Copyright © Pearson Education, Inc., or its affiliates. All Rights Reserved.

Core Concepts Part 9
Tools of History

Test B

Critical Thinking

12. What are two situations that may cause a primary source to be an unreliable account of what actually happened?

13. What might an artifact tell a historian about a society in the past?

14. What kinds of information might a historian learn from a community's oral tradition?

Essay

15. What type of historical information would a historical map show less effectively than another type of source would?

Name _____ Class _____ Date _____

CHAPTER 1

The United States

Test A

Key Terms
Complete each statement.

1. In general, the continental United States has a _____ climate.

2. Agricultural goods are the main _____ of the United States to other nations around the world.

Key Ideas
Identify the choice that best completes the statement or answers the question.

_____ 3. The highest elevations in the United States are located in
   a. the Sierra Nevada.
   b. the Great Plains.
   c. the Rocky Mountains.
   d. the coastal regions.

_____ 4. Which of the following doubled the size of the United States in 1803?
   a. The Civil War
   b. The Louisiana Purchase
   c. The American Revolution
   d. The Industrial Revolution

_____ 5. The Native American living in the _____ were most likely to use canoes.
   a. Eastern woodlands
   b. Great Basin
   c. Plains
   d. Southwest

_____ 6. Many immigrants were likely drawn to the United States because of the individual rights and freedoms guaranteed by the
   a. Constitution.
   b. doctrine of Manifest Destiny.
   c. civil rights movement.
   d. Industrial Revolution.

_____ 7. NAFTA is a trade agreement among
   a. the United States, China, and India.
   b. the United States, Canada, and Mexico.
   c. the United States, Japan, and Mexico.
   d. the United States, South America, and the Middle East.

_____ 8. The cultural diversity of the United States tends to be highest
   a. in the Midwest and central states.
   b. along the border with Canada.
   c. along the border with Mexico.
   d. in New England.

Copyright © Pearson Education, Inc., or its affiliates. All Rights Reserved.

Name _____ Class _____ Date _____

CHAPTER 1 — The United States — Test A

Critical Thinking

9. How might natural features help explain the lower population density of the western states?

10. How did the idea of Manifest Destiny affect Native Americans?

11. Why is diplomacy a key part of U.S. foreign policy?

Essay

12. Discuss the importance of immigration in shaping the United States. Give at least one example each of how immigration has influenced the nation's economy, culture, and population.

Name _____ Class _____ Date _____

CHAPTER 1

The United States — Test B

Key Terms
Complete each statement.

1. The United States has experienced a steady shift in population from the countryside to cities and _____, or areas in which several cities are geographically close together.

2. The United States has a _____, in which decisions on what to buy or sell are made by individuals and businesses, rather than by a centralized government or other authority.

Key Ideas
Identify the choice that best completes the statement or answers the question.

____ 3. Which of the following physical features attracted settlers who were looking for easier ways to travel?
   a. Rivers
   b. Mountains
   c. The Great Lakes
   d. The Great Plains

____ 4. Which of the following statements about the natural resources of the United States is most accurate?
   a. The many agricultural resources of the United States have made up for its lack of other resources.
   b. U.S. industry and agriculture have prospered because America has many different natural resources.
   c. The United States has had to import most of its resources from other nations elsewhere in the world.
   d. Natural resources such as clothing and cars have helped the U.S. economy.

____ 5. Many Italian and Polish immigrants came to the United States
   a. before the Civil War.
   b. in the early 1900s.
   c. in the late 1900s.
   d. since the 1960s.

____ 6. Native American cultures were disrupted when the Europeans arrived and introduced
   a. the idea of farming.
   b. unfamiliar diseases.
   c. fishing practices.
   d. dissenters.

____ 7. The forests of the Pacific Northwest are just one of the many different _____ in the United States where many people work in the same industry.
   a. elevation regions
   b. political regions
   c. climate regions
   d. economic regions

____ 8. The organization known as USAID
   a. promotes free trade.
   b. provides military aid.
   c. provides food aid.
   d. negotiates peace treaties.

Copyright © Pearson Education, Inc., or its affiliates. All Rights Reserved.

Name _____ Class _____ Date _____

CHAPTER 1
The United States   Test B

Critical Thinking

9. Compare and contrast the Appalachian Mountains and the Rocky Mountains.

_____
_____
_____
_____

10. In what ways was the civil rights movement a major change for African Americans?

_____
_____
_____
_____

11. Why might an immigrant want to become a U.S. citizen?

_____
_____
_____
_____

Essay

12. How has the cultural diversity of the United States changed over time? How is this change reflected in modern American society?

_____
_____
_____
_____
_____
_____
_____
_____
_____
_____

Copyright © Pearson Education, Inc., or its affiliates. All Rights Reserved.

Name _____ Class _____ Date _____

CHAPTER 2 Canada   Test A

Key Terms
Complete each statement.

1. The harsh _____ climate of Northern Canada has limited the population in the region.

2. The islands of the Arctic Archipelago contain _____, soil that remains frozen even when the summer warmth temporarily melts the snow and ice that usually covers the area.

3. The colony of _____ existed alongside British Canada for many years.

4. Modern Canada is a diverse society best described as a _____ of many people who keep their own cultural identities.

Key Ideas
Identify the choice that best completes the statement or answers the question.

____ 5. Where is the majority of Canada's oil found?
   a. Along the Atlantic Coast
   b. Along the border with the United States
   c. In western Canada
   d. Near the Arctic Ocean

____ 6. Where is Canada's population density highest?
   a. In the cities of Northern Canada
   b. In cities in central Canada
   c. In cities along the United States border
   d. In cities along the Atlantic and Pacific Coasts

____ 7. What natural resource most attracted European traders to Canada?
   a. Timber
   b. Animal furs
   c. Fish
   d. Whales

____ 8. Which of the following officials has the greatest amount of executive power in the Canadian government?
   a. Prime Minister
   b. Governor General
   c. Sovereign
   d. Supreme Court

____ 9. Canada currently ranks first in the world in which category?
   a. Total number of Internet users
   b. Percentage of college and university graduates
   c. Literacy rate of adult population
   d. Average unemployment among citizens

Copyright © Pearson Education, Inc., or its affiliates. All Rights Reserved.

Name _____ Class _____ Date _____

CHAPTER 2 Canada — Test A

Critical Thinking

10. How are Canada's settlement patterns similar to those of the United States?

_____
_____
_____
_____

11. How did Canada's growth affect its government and its ties to Great Britain?

_____
_____
_____
_____

12. If Canada had a less skilled workforce, what advantages would its economy still possess?

_____
_____
_____
_____

Essay

13. Did Britain's actions after the Seven Years' War help or hurt cooperation between Canada's different ethnic groups? Explain your answer, then tell how Canadian law addresses multiculturalism today.

_____
_____
_____
_____
_____
_____
_____
_____
_____
_____
_____
_____

Copyright © Pearson Education, Inc., or its affiliates. All Rights Reserved.

Name _____ Class _____ Date _____

CHAPTER 2 Canada   Test B

Key Terms
Complete each statement.

1. Canada's fishing industry benefits from the _____ where warm and cold waters combine in the Grand Banks.
2. The many lakes of the Canadian Shield region were created by _____, thick sheets of ice made of compacted snow.
3. In 1867, Canada became a _____ that governed itself but had its foreign affairs controlled by Great Britain.
4. The modern Canadian government is a _____ modeled on the government of Great Britain.

Key Ideas
Identify the choice that best completes the statement or answers the question.

____ 5. Most of Canada's border with the United States falls into which of Canada's six main climate regions?
   a. Semi-arid
   b. Maritime
   c. Continental warm summer
   d. Subarctic

____ 6. The people who first made use of the abundant resources of southern Canada were members of
   a. the First Nations.
   b. New France.
   c. British Canada.
   d. the Inuit.

____ 7. Britain guaranteed the rights of French Canadians in the
   a. Quebec Act of 1775.
   b. Act of Union.
   c. British North American Act.
   d. Dominion of Canada.

____ 8. Canada's most important trading partner is
   a. the United States.
   b. Mexico.
   c. the World Trade Organization.
   d. NATO.

____ 9. Canada has a bilingual government, which means
   a. every citizen is required to speak two languages.
   b. the country has two official languages, English and French.
   c. the country has two official languages, English and Spanish.
   d. all elected officials must be fluent in both English and French.

Copyright © Pearson Education, Inc., or its affiliates. All Rights Reserved.

Name _____ Class _____ Date _____

CHAPTER 2: Canada — Test B

Critical Thinking

10. Give two reasons why a majority of Canadians live in cities.

11. Compare and contrast the Dominion of Canada with the Canadian government after 1931.

12. How does international trade affect Canada's economy?

Essay

13. In what ways does cultural diversity benefit Canada? In what ways does this diversity pose a political and social challenge for Canada?

Name _____ Class _____ Date _____

CHAPTER 3 — Mexico — Test A

Key Terms
Complete each statement.

1. Differences in _____, or height above sea level, help to give Mexico a wide variety of climates.
2. The Aztecs supplied large cities with water by building _____, connecting the cities with sources of water in outlying areas.
3. The _____ began in 1910 and led to political and social reforms.
4. Mexico's economy began to grow after its leaders turned to _____ ideas.

Key Ideas
Identify the choice that best completes the statement or answers the question.

____ 5. Compared to southern Mexico, northern Mexico
  a. has a drier climate with less yearly rainfall.
  b. has fewer temperature changes during the year.
  c. suffers from more hurricanes during the summer and fall.
  d. has a higher population.

____ 6. Mexico's most important natural resource is
  a. gold.
  b. petroleum.
  c. coffee.
  d. corn.

____ 7. Mexico City was built by the
  a. Olmecs, when they began to grow maize.
  b. Mayans, after they conquered the Valley of Mexico.
  c. Spanish, on the ruins of the Aztec capital.
  d. Mexican government, after Mexico gained independence.

____ 8. How is Mexico's constitution different from the constitution of the United States?
  a. Mexico does not allow multiple political parties.
  b. Voters must be at least 21 years old.
  c. Eligible voters are required by law to vote in elections.
  d. Mexico has more than three branches of government.

____ 9. Which of the following best describes Mexico's economy?
  a. Mexico's economy depends mainly on oil production.
  b. The government tightly controls the Mexican economy.
  c. Mexico has one of the most productive economies in the world.
  d. Mexican workers earn the same as their American and Canadian counterparts.

Name _____ Class _____ Date _____

CHAPTER 3 Mexico — Test A

Critical Thinking

10. Where is most of Mexico's oil found, and why is this resource important to the country?

_____
_____
_____
_____

11. What were the short-term and long-term causes of the Mexican Revolution?

_____
_____
_____
_____

12. What encourages Mexican workers to come to the United States and how do these workers affect Mexico's economy?

_____
_____
_____
_____
_____

Essay

13. Compare the governments of the United States and Mexico. How has Mexico's political history differed from that of the United States?

_____
_____
_____
_____
_____
_____
_____
_____
_____
_____
_____

Name _____ Class _____ Date _____

CHAPTER 3 Mexico   Test B

Completion
Complete each statement.

1. Much of Mexico has a dry climate that farmers must _____ to help feed its growing population.
2. Hernan Cortés, who defeated the Aztec empire for the Spanish, was a _____, or soldier-explorer.
3. The PRI, or _____, ruled Mexico for most of the 1900s.
4. Many Mexicans work in the United States and send _____ back to Mexico to help support their families.

Key Ideas
Identify the choice that best completes the statement or answers the question.

____ 5. Sinkholes are found in the
   a. Mexican Plateau.
   b. Pacific Coastal Lowlands.
   c. Sierra Madres.
   d. Yucatan Peninsula.

____ 6. The first Native American civilization to arise in Mexico was the
   a. Olmec.
   b. Maya.
   c. Aztec.
   d. Yucatan.

____ 7. When did Mexico gain its independence from Spain?
   a. 1810
   b. 1821
   c. 1910
   d. 1917

____ 8. Which of the following statements best describes Mexican history?
   a. After Mexico gained independence, all land was taken from the wealthy and given to the poor.
   b. The Mexican people benefited greatly from foreign companies doing work in Mexico.
   c. After the Mexican Revolution, there were many reforms that helped the poor.
   d. Power and wealth remained in the hands of a small group, while many people remained poor.

____ 9. Most Mexican workers are employed in
   a. farming.
   b. manufacturing jobs.
   c. service industries.
   d. the oil industry.

Copyright © Pearson Education, Inc., or its affiliates. All Rights Reserved.

Name _____ Class _____ Date _____

CHAPTER 3 Mexico   Test B

Critical Thinking

10. How is Baja California similar to and different from the rest of Mexico?

_____
_____
_____
_____

11. How do the resources of Mexico's mountains and plateaus contribute to its economy?

_____
_____
_____
_____

12. How has Mexico's government changed in recent years?

_____
_____
_____
_____

Essay

13. Was Mexico's economy stronger or weaker when it depended mainly upon its natural resources? Explain your answer, describing Mexico's key natural resources and how its economy has changed today.

_____
_____
_____
_____
_____
_____
_____
_____
_____
_____
_____
_____

Copyright © Pearson Education, Inc., or its affiliates. All Rights Reserved.

Name _____ Class _____ Date _____

CHAPTER 4
Central America and the Caribbean
Test A

Key Terms

Complete each statement.

1. _____ is the business of providing food, places to stay, and other services to visitors from other places.

2. Ranching and farming led to _____, or the removal of a large number of trees from an area.

3. Around 1000 B.C., Native Americans known as the _____ began settling in what is now Guatemala.

4. _____ combines Catholic and West African beliefs.

5. An increase in _____, or tourism that focuses on the environment, has led to more people exploring the region on foot or on horseback.

Key Ideas

Identify the choice that best completes the statement or answers the question.

____ 6. A tropical climate is key to which economic activity in the lowlands of Central America and the Caribbean?
  a. Commerce and manufacturing
  b. Production of cash crops, such as sugar and coffee
  c. Livestock raising
  d. Mining

____ 7. The group of Native Americans who settled what is now Guatemala were
  a. the Creoles.
  b. the Aztecs.
  c. the Olmecs.
  d. the Maya.

____ 8. Sugar, African slaves, rum, tobacco, and molasses formed a triangular system of trade connecting the Caribbean with
  a. Europe and Africa.
  b. Europe and Central America.
  c. Central America and Africa.
  d. Africa and South America.

____ 9. Foreigners continued to have influence after independence because they
  a. maintained military bases within each country.
  b. provided the investment to help build the countries' economies.
  c. advised the presidents of the new countries.
  d. controlled trade through the colonial system.

____ 10. Most governments in Central America are
  a. dictatorships.
  b. parliamentary democracies.
  c. presidential democracies.
  d. free trade associations.

Name _____ Class _____ Date _____

CHAPTER 4
Central America and the Caribbean

Test A

Critical Thinking

11. What was the encomienda system?

12. What is one cause of the diaspora of Central American and Caribbean people?

13. How is ecotourism different from traditional tourism?

Essay

14. Did independence in Central America and the Caribbean bring real change to the region or not? Explain your answer.

Name _____ Class _____ Date _____

CHAPTER 4
Central America and the Caribbean

Test B

Key Terms

Complete each statement.

1. Caribbean islands have great _____, a wide variety of living things.

2. In Spanish colonies, the _____ system was established, which controlled the Native American population in the Spanish colonies.

3. A government controlled by a single leader is a _____.

4. Poor farmers can sometimes get small loans called _____ to start their own farms.

5. _____ is a religious festival in late winter and is primarily observed by Roman Catholics.

Key Ideas

Identify the choice that best completes the statement or answers the question.

____ 6. Tourism is popular in Central America and the Caribbean largely because of the region's
   a. hurricanes.
   b. dry, cool highland climate.
   c. earthquakes.
   d. tropical climate.

____ 7. Before the arrival of the Europeans, the Caribbean islands were settled by
   a. the Aztec and the Olmec.
   b. the Arawak and the Carib.
   c. the Creole and the Maya.
   d. conquistadors.

____ 8. How did European colonists in Central America and the Caribbean deal with the huge amounts of land and labor required to grow cash crops?
   a. They imported Native Americans.
   b. They exported other crops that did not require so much land and labor.
   c. They exported enslaved Africans.
   d. They imported enslaved Africans.

____ 9. Which country has the region's most stable democracy?
   a. Guatemala
   b. Costa Rica
   c. Haiti
   d. Dominican Republic

____ 10. Which is a language that combines French and African influences?
   a. Creole
   b. Spanish
   c. Achi
   d. Quechua

Copyright © Pearson Education, Inc., or its affiliates. All Rights Reserved.
63

Name _____ Class _____ Date _____

CHAPTER 4
Central America and the Caribbean

Test B

Critical Thinking

11. Why might people have different viewpoints on whether tourism is good or bad for Central America and the Caribbean?

_____
_____
_____
_____

12. How might people in the newly independent countries of Central America and the Caribbean have disagreed over the influence of foreign powers in their countries?

_____
_____
_____
_____

13. What are two effects of the diaspora of Central American and Caribbean people?

_____
_____
_____

Essay

14. What were the effects of colonization on Central America and the Caribbean?

_____
_____
_____
_____
_____
_____
_____
_____
_____
_____
_____

Copyright © Pearson Education, Inc., or its affiliates. All Rights Reserved.

Name _____ Class _____ Date _____

CHAPTER 5
Caribbean South America

Test A

Key Terms
Complete each statement.

1. The three parallel ranges of the Andes Mountains in Columbia are known as _____.

2. After independence, _____, or dictators, soon emerged to control the governments.

3. In 1989 the government of Venezuela introduced _____, or policies meant to save money, to try to bring an end to economic decline.

4. Venezuela suffers from land _____, or the sinking of the ground, caused by decades of draining the underground oilfields.

5. In Colombia, the government has been fighting a civil war against _____, or rebels, for decades.

6. When the Venezuelan government took control of the country's oil industry in 1976, it _____ that industry.

Key Ideas
Identify the choice that best completes the statement or answers the question.

____ 7. What natural resource is concentrated around Lake Maracaibo in Venezuela?
   a. Natural gas
   b. Silver
   c. Oil
   d. Gold

____ 8. In Guyana and Suriname, the dominant ethnic group is made up of people descended from workers who migrated from
   a. India.
   b. China.
   c. Africa.
   d. France.

____ 9. In Caribbean South America, which countries are most influenced by Spanish culture?
   a. Colombia and Venezuela
   b. Guyana, Suriname, and French Guiana
   c. Colombia and Guyana
   d. Suriname and Venezuela

____ 10. In Suriname, the most common languages spoken are
   a. Italian and Greek.
   b. English, Dutch, and Surinamese.
   c. French, Spanish, and Surinamese.
   d. Spanish, Portuguese, and Surinamese.

Name _____ Class _____ Date _____

CHAPTER 5
Caribbean South America

Test A

Critical Thinking

11. What were two ways in which European colonists changed the physical geography of Caribbean South America?

_____
_____
_____
_____

12. How do landforms influence where different kinds of people live in the Andes and the Pampas?

_____
_____
_____
_____

13. What effect has oil had on Venezuela's economy?

_____
_____
_____
_____

Essay

14. How well does the term "Latin America" describe the region of Caribbean South America? Explain your answer.

_____
_____
_____
_____
_____
_____
_____
_____
_____
_____

Copyright © Pearson Education, Inc., or its affiliates. All Rights Reserved.

Name _____ Class _____ Date _____

CHAPTER 5
Caribbean South America
Test B

Key Terms

Complete each statement.

1. The plants and animals that depend on each other and their environment for survival is called a(n) _____.

2. Sculpting a hillside into different flat areas suitable for growing crops is known as _____.

3. The Spanish hunted for treasure and a legendary gold-rich king called _____ in Caribbean South America.

4. Armed forces that are unauthorized by the government are called _____.

5. The form of democracy in which the people elect representatives to make the nation's laws is called _____.

6. The parts of the American continents that have been heavily influenced by the cultures of Spain, France, and Portugal are called _____.

Key Ideas

Identify the choice that best completes the statement or answers the question.

____ 7. Most of Colombia's people live
   a. along the coast.
   b. in the mountains.
   c. in the east.
   d. on the border with Venezuela.

____ 8. Who liberated the lands that later became the countries of Colombia and Venezuela?
   a. The *caudillos*
   b. Simón Bolívar
   c. The peninsulares
   d. Carlos Andrés Pérez

____ 9. After liberation from Spain, the new countries of South America were ruled primarily by
   a. freed slaves.
   b. a small minority from the upper classes.
   c. indigenous peoples.
   d. the British.

____ 10. In which country is the main language English?
   a. Colombia
   b. Venezuela
   c. Guyana
   d. Suriname

Copyright © Pearson Education, Inc., or its affiliates. All Rights Reserved.

Name _____ Class _____ Date _____

CHAPTER 5: Caribbean South America

Test B

Critical Thinking

11. What makes the highlands of the Andes a good place to grow many types of crops?

_____
_____
_____
_____

12. Why might some people in colonial Caribbean South America have fought against Simón Bolívar?

_____
_____
_____
_____

13. How might Guyana benefit from offshore oil in the future?

_____
_____
_____
_____

Essay

14. How has the geography of Caribbean South America affected settlement and population in the region over time?

_____
_____
_____
_____
_____
_____
_____
_____
_____
_____
_____
_____
_____
_____

Name _____ Class _____ Date _____

CHAPTER 6
The Andes and the Pampas

Test A

Key Terms
Complete each statement.

1. Mountain ranges such as the Andes are formed when one tectonic plate is _____, or pulled underneath another.

2. _____ is a regular weather event that can cause heavy rain in the Andes and Pampas.

3. So many Incans died from disease because they lacked _____.

4. After Argentina won independence, a(n) _____ was formed to govern the country.

5. Both crops and corporations help Peru to have a more _____.

Key Ideas
Identify the choice that best completes the statement or answers the question.

____ 6. In a vertical climate zone, where would you find the coldest, wettest climate?
   a. At the lowest point
   b. At the highest point
   c. In the middle
   d. There are no cold, wet climates in a vertical climate zone.

____ 7. The Altiplano is a high, flat area in the Andes filled with
   a. natural resources.
   b. crops.
   c. vertical climate zones.
   d. people.

____ 8. One of the Europeans' strongest weapons against the Incas was
   a. surprise attacks.
   b. trained soldiers.
   c. disease.
   d. horses.

____ 9. At the top of the class system during Spanish colonial times were those born in Spain, who were known as
   a. criollos.
   b. peninsulares.
   c. mestizos.
   d. gauchos.

____ 10. An important tool used to strengthen the democracies of the Andes and Pampas is
   a. literacy.
   b. corruption.
   c. referendum.
   d. environmental policies.

Copyright © Pearson Education, Inc., or its affiliates. All Rights Reserved.

Name _____ Class _____ Date _____

CHAPTER 6
The Andes and the Pampas

Test A

Critical Thinking

11. Why is Buenos Aires different from other parts in the region in terms of population density?

_____
_____
_____

12. Following independence, how were events in Chile and Argentina similar?

_____
_____
_____
_____

13. What is the link between European influence and cultural diversity in the Andes and the Pampas?

_____
_____
_____
_____

Essay

14. Predict how ethnic diversity in the region will continue to influence the governments of different countries.

_____
_____
_____
_____
_____
_____
_____
_____
_____
_____
_____

Name _____ Class _____ Date _____

CHAPTER 6
The Andes and the Pampas

Test B

Key Terms
Complete each statement.

1. Farmers make use of _____ to grow different crops at different heights in the Andes.

2. An area in the Andes that is rich in silver and tin is the _____.

3. _____ were people who had European fathers and indigenous mothers.

4. The system called _____ made colonies dependent on Spain.

5. _____ is a country whose president is a Native American who champions social movements.

Key Ideas
Identify the choice that best completes the statement or answers the question.

____ 6. What phenomenon influences the climate of the Andes and the Pampas every few years?
   a. Vertical climate zones
   b. Cordilleras
   c. Human activity
   d. El Niño

____ 7. The Andes and the Pampas have a wide range of ecosystems because of
   a. desertification.
   b. deforestation.
   c. the effects of altitude.
   d. globalization.

____ 8. Which empire was the largest in the Americas in the 1400s?
   a. The Pampas
   b. The Incas
   c. The Peninsulares
   d. The Mestizos

____ 9. In the 1970s, political unrest that began with the overthrow of President Allende occurred in the country of
   a. Chile.
   b. Uruguay.
   c. Argentina.
   d. Paraguay.

____ 10. _____ is both good and bad for the countries in the Andes and the Pampas.
   a. Literacy
   b. Deforestation
   c. Referendum
   d. Globalization

Copyright © Pearson Education, Inc., or its affiliates. All Rights Reserved.

Name _____ Class _____ Date _____

CHAPTER 6
The Andes and the Pampas

Test B

Critical Thinking

11. What are the two largest groups of people who live in the Andes and Pampas?

12. What conclusion can be drawn about the early civilizations that developed in the Andes and the Pampas?

13. What conclusion can you draw about the system of mercantilism set up by Spain?

Essay

14. Summarize how the economic history of the Andes and the Pampas influences the economies of countries in the region today.

Name _____ Class _____ Date _____

CHAPTER 7 Brazil   Test A

Key Terms

Complete each statement.

1. The _____ is the land drained by the Amazon River.
2. The outskirts of Brazilian cities are filled with slums called _____.
3. A(n) _____ economy is based on sending goods to other nations.
4. People who wanted to end slavery were called _____.
5. _____, a fuel that can be made form sugar cane, is allowing Brazil to reduce its dependence on oil.
6. Brazil has a(n) _____, in which the prices of goods are set by demand, not by the government.

Key Ideas

Identify the choice that best completes the statement or answers the question.

____ 7. What type of land covers over half the country of Brazil?
   a. Grassland
   b. Farmland
   c. Forest
   d. Wetland

____ 8. Why did the Portuguese first bring enslaved Africans to Brazil?
   a. To trade with them for brazilwood
   b. To work on sugar plantations
   c. To work on coffee plantations
   d. To work in gold and diamond mines

____ 9. The first emperor of Brazil was
   a. a general who led a coup against the Portuguese.
   b. a wealthy coffee-grower.
   c. a native who seized power from the Europeans.
   d. the son of the king of Portugal.

____ 10. What is the festival celebrated in Brazil with several days of parades, music, and dance, which combines religious traditions of southern Europe with the music and dance of Africa and the Americas?
   a. Capoeira
   b. Lent
   c. Carnival
   d. Curitiba

____ 11. Brazil's membership in MERCOSUR means that it
   a. sends peacekeeping troops to war-torn areas of the continent.
   b. will provide economic aid to developing nations.
   c. is committed to free trade with neighboring countries.
   d. works with other oil exporters to set prices and control production.

Copyright © Pearson Education, Inc., or its affiliates. All Rights Reserved.

Name _____ Class _____ Date _____

CHAPTER 7 Brazil Test A

Critical Thinking

12. What type of climate supports Brazil's huge rain forest?
_____
_____
_____

13. How did a boom in Brazil's coffee production help lead to changes in the country's government in the late 1800s?
_____
_____
_____
_____

14. What are some benefits and drawbacks to cutting down trees in the Amazon rain forest?
_____
_____
_____
_____

Essay

15. Why has it been so difficult to stop destruction of the Amazon rain forest, and what else might be done to stop it?
_____
_____
_____
_____
_____
_____
_____
_____
_____

Copyright © Pearson Education, Inc., or its affiliates. All Rights Reserved.

Name _____ Class _____ Date _____

CHAPTER 7 Brazil — Test B

Key Terms

Complete each statement.

1. A parklike landscape of grasslands is called a(n) _____.
2. The upper level of rain forest trees, called the _____, prevents most of the sun's rays from reaching the ground.
3. An overthrow of the government is called a(n) _____.
4. Curitiba has reduced car traffic and trash while creating a parklike environment through careful _____.
5. A period of rapid economic growth followed by a sharp downturn is called a _____ and _____ cycle.
6. Programs designed to help the poor are called _____.

Key Ideas

Identify the choice that best completes the statement or answers the question.

____ 7. The largest city in Brazil is
   a. Brasilia.
   b. Manaus.
   c. Rio de Janeiro.
   d. São Paulo.

____ 8. What kind of economy did the Portuguese set up in Brazil?
   a. A boom economy
   b. An import economy
   c. A bust economy
   d. An export economy

____ 9. Where does African heritage remain strongest in Brazil?
   a. In the rain forests
   b. Along the northeast coast
   c. Along the southeast coast
   d. In the Brazilian highlands

____ 10. Today, Brazil's economy is best described as
   a. a market economy.
   b. a command economy.
   c. a mixed economy.
   d. an export economy.

____ 11. Which of the following is the same when comparing the political system in Brazil to that of the United States?
   a. An executive branch headed by a president
   b. A minimum voting age of 21
   c. A Congress with three houses
   d. A legislature that decides court cases

Copyright © Pearson Education, Inc., or its affiliates. All Rights Reserved.

Name _____ Class _____ Date _____

CHAPTER 7 Brazil — Test B

Critical Thinking

12. How does the Amazon rain forest's location on the equator affect its climate?

_____
_____
_____

13. What effect did a series of booms and busts have on Brazil's economy?

_____
_____
_____

14. What steps is Brazil taking to deal with pollution?

_____
_____
_____

Essay

15. Did Portuguese colonization bring bigger changes to the physical or human geography of Brazil? Explain your answer.

_____
_____
_____
_____
_____
_____
_____
_____
_____
_____

Copyright © Pearson Education, Inc., or its affiliates. All Rights Reserved.

Name _____ Class _____ Date _____

CHAPTER 8
Ancient and Medieval Europe

Test A

Key Terms

Complete each statement.

1. Under the statesman Pericles, Athens became the world's first _____, or government in which citizens take part directly in the day-to-day affairs of government.

2. The two main groups in the Roman republic were the _____, or the wealthy aristocrats, and the plebeians, or all the remaining citizens.

3. The period of stability known as the _____, which lasted for about 200 years, began under the rule of Augustus.

4. Feudalism is the system of mutual rights and duties that connect _____ and _____ to each other.

5. The _____ were a series of military expeditions to take the Holy Land from the Muslims.

Key Ideas

Identify the choice that best completes the statement or answers the question.

_____ 6. As trade helped spread Greek culture and brought other cultures to Greece, it became a _____, or center of new ideas.
   a. colony
   b. cultural hearth
   c. oligarchy
   d. peninsula

_____ 7. During the time of the Roman republic, the tribunes played a crucial role in the government by
   a. representing the rights of the plebeians.
   b. recruiting soldiers for the army.
   c. reporting the news in the marketplace.
   d. passing laws for all citizens.

_____ 8. One difference between the Christian church in the east and the Christian church in the west was that priests in the eastern Church
   a. were not allowed to marry.
   b. reported to the patriarch of Rome.
   c. could marry.
   d. spoke Latin instead of Greek.

_____ 9. The Magna Carta was the first step toward England's
   a. large cities.
   b. war with France.
   c. merchant guilds.
   d. more democratic government.

Copyright © Pearson Education, Inc., or its affiliates. All Rights Reserved.

Name _____ Class _____ Date _____

CHAPTER 8
Ancient and Medieval Europe

Test A

Critical Thinking

10. How did geography play a part in shaping Greek civilization, especially city-states?

_____
_____
_____
_____

11. How did Charlemagne change Europe?

_____
_____
_____
_____

12. Why were Italian trade centers important?

_____
_____
_____
_____

Essay

13. What was the classical period of Greece and what were some of the achievements in art, science, and philosophy made during this period?

_____
_____
_____
_____
_____
_____
_____
_____
_____
_____
_____
_____

Name _____ Class _____ Date _____

CHAPTER 8
Ancient and Medieval Europe

Test B

Key Terms

Complete each statement.

1. The fortified towns built by the Mycenaeans gradually developed into _____, which are cities or towns that control nearby areas.

2. Greeks studied _____ to try to understand their world through logic and reason.

3. The Ancient Roman government was a _____ democracy, where citizens elect other citizens to make political decisions for them.

4. Following the Great _____, or split, of 1054, the Byzantine church became the Eastern (or Greek) Orthodox Church.

5. The primary difference between the concepts of feudalism and manorialism is that feudalism was a legal relationship, and that manorialism was a(n) _____ system.

Key Ideas

Identify the choice that best completes the statement or answers the question.

____ 6. Greece's economy prospered thanks to
   a. the arts.
   b. philosophy.
   c. trade.
   d. architecture.

____ 7. In Athens, the system of government became a direct democracy, in which the people participated directly in government. In the Roman republic, citizens participated in government
   a. in the exact same way.
   b. through meetings held in the marketplace.
   c. by taking turns serving as consul.
   d. by choosing representatives who made decisions and laws.

____ 8. Compasses and _____ were two new technologies that Europe gained from contact with the Muslim world.
   a. clocks
   b. astrolabes
   c. cannons
   d. eyeglasses

____ 9. Nation-building began in Europe as a result of war and the
   a. end of Muslim rule.
   b. growth of cities.
   c. Black Death.
   d. Magna Carta.

Copyright © Pearson Education, Inc., or its affiliates. All Rights Reserved.

Name _____ Class _____ Date _____

CHAPTER 8
Ancient and Medieval Europe

Test B

Critical Thinking

10. What event happened in A.D. 312 that sped up the spread of Christianity in the Roman Empire?

_____
_____
_____
_____

11. In what ways did the Christian church play a key role in medieval life?

_____
_____
_____
_____

12. How did the Black Death affect Europe?

_____
_____
_____
_____

Essay

13. What do you think were the most important reasons the Romans could grow from shepherd villages in central Italy into a mighty global empire?

_____
_____
_____
_____
_____
_____
_____
_____
_____
_____
_____
_____

Name _____ Class _____ Date _____

CHAPTER 9
Europe in Modern Times

Test A

Key Terms
Complete each statement.

1. The artistic technique that allows artists to portray a three-dimensional space on a flat surface is called _____.

2. Explorers searched for the _____, or route between the Atlantic and the Pacific along the northern coast of North America.

3. At first, the Industrial Revolution brought pollution, long working hours, _____, and poor living conditions to society.

4. At the end of World War I, the Allies forced Germany to sign the _____, which humiliated and angered Germany.

5. During the late 1900s, a global economy developed as foreign trade and _____ grew.

Key Ideas
Identify the choice that best completes the statement or answers the question.

____ 6. The philosophy that emphasizes individual accomplishment and serving the people of this world as opposed to focusing on religion is known as
   a. humanism.
   b. reformation.
   c. perspective.
   d. classical influence.

____ 7. Advances in science from the Scientific Revolution were applied to human affairs during the
   a. Industrial Revolution.
   b. French Revolution.
   c. Enlightenment.
   d. Age of Exploration.

____ 8. During the Great Depression, the United States put tariffs on imported farm products to protect the country's
   a. stock markets.
   b. investors.
   c. farmers.
   d. banks.

____ 9. By 2008, 27 countries were members of the
   a. European Union.
   b. Marshall Plan.
   c. Iron Curtain.
   d. Soviet Union.

Copyright © Pearson Education, Inc., or its affiliates. All Rights Reserved.

Name _____ Class _____ Date _____

CHAPTER 9 **Europe in Modern Times** **Test A**

Critical Thinking

10. How did Renaissance thinkers and the Scientific Revolution help start the Enlightenment?
_____
_____
_____

11. How did the Industrial Revolution change European industry and trade?
_____
_____
_____

12. Why did many Germans accept Hitler and Nazi Party rule?
_____
_____
_____
_____

Essay

13. Europe faces major challenges, such as strengthening the economies of Eastern Europe, the global economy, international terrorism, migration, and energy and the environment. Which of these challenges do you think will be the most difficult to meet? Why?
_____
_____
_____
_____
_____
_____
_____
_____
_____
_____
_____

Name _____ Class _____ Date _____

CHAPTER 9
Europe in Modern Times
Test B

Key Terms
Complete each statement.

1. Johannes Gutenberg perfected _____, which made his printing press possible.

2. The three-stage pattern of Atlantic trade between Europe, Africa, and the Americas is called _____.

3. Renaissance thinkers relied on _____ to explain the world.

4. The political system that stresses national strength, military might, and the idea that the state is more important than individuals is _____.

5. Mikhail Gorbachev loosened government control in the Soviet Union and supported greater _____ in the Soviet satellite nations of Eastern Europe.

Key Ideas
Identify the choice that best completes the statement or answers the question.

____ 6. After the Protestant Reformation, the Catholic church began to respond to the reformers' criticisms by beginning the
   a. Inquisition.
   b. Secular Reformation.
   c. 95 Theses.
   d. Catholic Reformation.

____ 7. The combination of scientific ideas from the Scientific Revolution and political ideas from the Enlightenment led to a period of social upheaval and
   a. colonial expansion.
   b. violent change.
   c. industrial expansion.
   d. absolutist monarchs.

____ 8. Thomas Newcomen and James Watt both invented
   a. electric light bulbs.
   b. gravity detectors.
   c. navigation instruments.
   d. steam engines.

____ 9. A visible symbol of the Cold War division between East and West was the
   a. Soviet Union.
   b. Marshall Plan.
   c. United Nations.
   d. Berlin Wall.

Copyright © Pearson Education, Inc., or its affiliates. All Rights Reserved.

Name _____ Class _____ Date _____

CHAPTER 9
Europe in Modern Times

Test B

Critical Thinking

10. What was the Columbian Exchange?

_____
_____
_____
_____

11. Why were antidemocratic leaders able to take power in the Soviet Union and Italy after World War I?

_____
_____
_____
_____

12. How was Europe divided after World War II and during the Cold War?

_____
_____
_____
_____

Essay

13. What is the relationship between the Age of Empire and World War 1?

_____
_____
_____
_____
_____
_____
_____
_____
_____
_____
_____
_____

Copyright © Pearson Education, Inc., or its affiliates. All Rights Reserved.

Name _____ Class _____ Date _____

CHAPTER 10 Western Europe — Test A

Key Terms
Complete each statement.

1. A thick forest of coniferous trees, called a _____, is found in areas such as Scandinavia.

2. Acid rain is one effect of _____.

3. Britain's use of the _____ as its currency instead of the euro shows that Britain prefers limited ties to the European Union.

4. The _____ ensures that French products, such as wine, cheese, and grains, reach people around the world.

5. The Southern European nations of Spain, Andorra, and Portugal are located on the _____.

6. Portugal's economic growth since it joined the EU is largely the result of Portugal's efforts to _____ its economy.

Key Ideas
Identify the choice that best completes the statement or answers the question.

____ 7. What made the Rhine River one of Europe's most polluted rivers?
   a. Urbanization
   b. Loess
   c. Industrial waste
   d. Natural gas

____ 8. Some Norwegians feel that the EU's structure is not democratic. As a result, these people probably favor _____ ties with the European Union.
   a. cultural
   b. democratic
   c. stronger
   d. limited

____ 9. Which of the following is the correct term for converting government-owned industries to private ownership?
   a. Reunification
   b. Privatization
   c. Gross national product
   d. Neutrality

____ 10. Which of the following industries is an example of the part of the economy known as the service sector?
   a. Telecommunications
   b. Textile production
   c. Computer chip manufacturing
   d. Porcelain production

Copyright © Pearson Education, Inc., or its affiliates. All Rights Reserved.

Name _____ Class _____ Date _____

CHAPTER 10 Western Europe — Test A

Critical Thinking

11. Why are Western Europe's most heavily populated areas within 100 miles of the coast?

_____
_____
_____

12. How does warm water brought to Europe's western coast by the Atlantic Ocean affect the region's climate?

_____
_____
_____

13. Why are many Germans both proud and uneasy about their culture?

_____
_____
_____

Essay

14. What problems does immigration cause in Europe, and how might European countries deal with these problems?

_____
_____
_____
_____
_____
_____
_____
_____
_____
_____

Copyright © Pearson Education, Inc., or its affiliates. All Rights Reserved.

Name _____ Class _____ Date _____

CHAPTER 10 Western Europe — Test B

Key Terms
Complete each statement.

1. In order to preserve land for forests, recreation, and growing food, most countries limit the growth of _____.

2. _____ is the total value of all goods and services produced and sold in a country in a year.

3. When the Berlin Wall fell in 1989, East Germany and West Germany began the process of _____.

4. Switzerland has a long history of _____, which has led to Switzerland's difficult relationships with international organizations.

5. Granada, Spain, which blends Christian, Jewish, and Muslim traditions, is an example of _____, or the spread of culture.

6. The process of sending an immigrant back to his or her home country is called _____.

Key Ideas
Identify the choice that best completes the statement or answers the question.

____ 7. Which feature of Western Europe helps make public transportation networks possible?
   a. Temperate climate
   b. Pollution
   c. Rich farmland
   d. Large urban areas

____ 8. What is the system of government in England called?
   a. House of Commons and House of Lords
   b. Constitutional monarchy
   c. Democracy
   d. British Constitution

____ 9. What industry is one of West Central Europe's largest and most important industries?
   a. Skiing
   b. Tourism
   c. Electrical machinery
   d. Book publishing

____ 10. The nations of Southern Europe have enjoyed strong growth as members of
   a. the European Union.
   b. NATO.
   c. Mediterranean culture.
   d. different religious groups.

Name _____ Class _____ Date _____

CHAPTER 10 Western Europe — Test B

Critical Thinking

11. Compare and contrast Western Europe's Arctic climate to its Mediterranean climate.

12. How does Germany's past affect the attitudes of today's Germans toward immigration and immigrants?

13. Discuss some of the reasons for economic changes experienced by Southern European countries.

Essay

14. In general, has membership in the European Union helped or hurt the countries of Western Europe?

Copyright © Pearson Education, Inc., or its affiliates. All Rights Reserved.

Name _____ Class _____ Date _____

CHAPTER 11 Eastern Europe — Test A

Key Terms
Complete each statement.

1. The physical features of this region were shaped by a long period of lower temperatures, when much of the land was covered in snow and ice. This period is known as a(n) _____.

2. Estonia's economy has been successful because its industries have _____, or money to invest.

3. Many republics in Yugoslavia were unhappy with the Serbian government, so they began to _____, or break away, from Yugoslavia.

Key Ideas
Identify the choice that best completes the statement or answers the question.

____ 4. As they moved, glaciers scraped up rocks and soil and then dropped these materials when they melted, creating _____ across the region.
   a. the North European Plain
   b. ridges of hills
   c. many large rivers
   d. the Carpathian Mountains

____ 5. Mechanized farming techniques are well-suited to geographic areas that
   a. have a shortage of inexpensive labor.
   b. are closer to major urban areas.
   c. have large expanses of flat land.
   d. experience frequent flooding.

____ 6. One reason why many people in Eastern Europe do not belong to any religion is that
   a. missionaries have been unable to reach the area.
   b. they are more concerned with Communist Party matters.
   c. religion was discouraged by the Soviet Union's government.
   d. economic hardship has made the people bitter.

____ 7. The Polish economy began to grow in the 1990s because the government
   a. built more state-owned factories.
   b. controlled prices better.
   c. stopped new private businesses.
   d. encouraged entrepreneurs.

____ 8. One of the worst ethnic conflicts, involving the policy of ethnic cleansing, was the war between Serbia and the province of
   a. Macedonia.   c. Montenegro.
   b. Kosovo.   d. Slovenia.

Copyright © Pearson Education, Inc., or its affiliates. All Rights Reserved.

Name _____ Class _____ Date _____

CHAPTER 11 Eastern Europe —— Test A

Critical Thinking

9. How has the fall of the Soviet Union changed attitudes toward religion in some Eastern European countries?

10. How is farming in the northern part of Eastern Europe different from farming in the southern part of the region?

11. Why is membership in the European Union so important to most of the Eastern European countries today?

Essay

12. What is the energy challenge facing Eastern Europe? If one of the Eastern European presidents asked you for advice, what would you recommend as a solution?

Copyright © Pearson Education, Inc., or its affiliates. All Rights Reserved.

Name _____ Class _____ Date _____

CHAPTER 11
Eastern Europe — Test B

Key Terms
Complete each statement.

1. Since the 1940s there has been a revival of Jewish communities in some areas, while, in other areas, Jewish people continue to _____, or leave one area to move to another.

2. Burning coal and other fossil fuels sends chemicals into the air, and this plays a part in the production of _____.

3. Hungarians, who are different in some ways from their Eastern European neighbors, have a unique _____, or style of food.

Key Ideas
Identify the choice that best completes the statement or answers the question.

____ 4. The 1986 explosion at the Chernobyl nuclear power plant in _____ caused a serious environmental problem.
   a. Poland
   b. Moldova
   c. Ukraine
   d. Belarus

____ 5. Most of Eastern Europe has very cold winters and mild summers, which is typical of the _____ climate.
   a. Mediterranean
   b. humid subtropical
   c. continental cool summer
   d. continental warm summer

____ 6. A nation whose industries have enough capital will be able to expand its economy because
   a. the business of the nation's government will take place in a single city.
   b. it can invest in equipment to make more goods for trade.
   c. service-sector industries will decrease in importance.
   d. the industries can overrule tariffs.

____ 7. The first republic to secede from the country of Yugoslavia in 1990 was
   a. Slovenia.
   b. Macedonia.
   c. Croatia.
   d. Slovakia.

____ 8. A consequence of the break-up of the country of Yugoslavia into different republics was
   a. the rise of a strong authoritarian regime aimed at re-uniting them.
   b. the founding of NATO to combat the new threat.
   c. ethnic cleansing and other efforts to create areas of only one ethnic group.
   d. enhanced trade between the new countries.

Copyright © Pearson Education, Inc., or its affiliates. All Rights Reserved.

Name _____ Class _____ Date _____

CHAPTER 11 Eastern Europe   Test B

Critical Thinking

9. In Eastern Europe, how does geography influence industry?
_____
_____
_____
_____

10. Why have Poland and the Baltic nations been among the most economically successful countries in Eastern Europe?
_____
_____
_____
_____

11. What has been the impact of ethnic conflict on the Balkan nations?
_____
_____
_____
_____
_____

Essay

12. If you were an entrepreneur, which of the Eastern European countries might be the best place to start your new business? Explain your reasoning.
_____
_____
_____
_____
_____
_____
_____
_____
_____
_____
_____
_____

Copyright © Pearson Education, Inc., or its affiliates. All Rights Reserved.

Name _____ Class _____ Date _____

CHAPTER 12 Russia — Test A

Key Terms
Complete each statement.

1. Famous for its 29 active volcanoes, the _____ lies at the eastern edge of the Russian Far East.

2. South of Moscow, the countryside consists mainly of vast areas of grassland, also known as _____.

3. Vladimir Lenin led to power a branch of the Social Democrats called the _____ and introduced communism.

4. Many believe the source of Putin's authoritative style is his involvement with the Soviet era secret police, known as the _____.

5. Russia is using its status as a(n) _____, or an extremely powerful nation, and its wealth of natural resources to be an important player on the world stage.

Key Ideas
Identify the choice that best completes the statement or answers the question.

____ 6. As a result of its vast reserves of _____, Russia has become a wealthy nation in recent years.
   a. timber
   b. coal
   c. oil and gas
   d. cobalt

____ 7. East Slavs who migrated to the Dnieper region encountered invaders from Asia, including Huns, Avars, Magyars, and
   a. Vikings.
   b. Finns.
   c. Goths.
   d. Khazars.

____ 8. Real reform in the Soviet Union began under _____, who introduced the policies of glasnost and perestroika.
   a. Vladimir Lenin
   b. Josef Stalin
   c. Mikhail Gorbachev
   d. Vladimir Putin

____ 9. During his terms in office, Vladimir Putin has made changes that have resulted in Russia becoming the world leader in
   a. personal income growth.
   b. reducing crime.
   c. the production of oil and gas.
   d. reducing poverty.

Copyright © Pearson Education, Inc., or its affiliates. All Rights Reserved.

Name _____ Class _____ Date _____

CHAPTER 12 Russia   Test A

Critical Thinking

10. How are climate and population density in Russia related?
_____
_____
_____

11. How did the Communists come to power in Russia?
_____
_____
_____
_____

12. Compare and contrast the way communism works with the way democratic capitalism works. Include the roles of the government, political leadership, and who makes political decisions.
_____
_____
_____
_____

Essay

13. How did the practice of communism in Russia differ from the theory of how communism is supposed to work?
_____
_____
_____
_____
_____
_____
_____
_____
_____
_____
_____

Copyright © Pearson Education, Inc., or its affiliates. All Rights Reserved.

Name _____ Class _____ Date _____

CHAPTER 12 Russia — Test B

Key Terms
Complete each statement.

1. The largest part of Russia, which is called _____, stretches eastward from the Ural Mountains to the Pacific Ocean.

2. Prince Ivan III began calling himself _____, a term derived from the Latin *Caesar* or king.

3. During the Russian revolution, Lenin and the Bolsheviks used Marx's ideas to gain the support of workers' councils known as _____, so Lenin could claim the Bolsheviks represented the voices of the working class.

4. Josef Stalin wanted agriculture to be controlled by groups instead of by individuals, a policy known as _____.

5. One of the powers of government that the Russian government exercises is to _____, or suppress, news stories that it does not like.

Key Ideas
Identify the choice that best completes the statement or answers the question.

___ 6. European Russia is separated from Asiatic Russia by the
   a. West Siberian Plain.
   b. Caucasus Mountains.
   c. Ural Mountains.
   d. Caspian Sea.

___ 7. Most of Russia's densely settled areas lie _____ of the Ural Mountains; most of the rest of Russia is sparsely populated.
   a. east
   b. west
   c. north
   d. south

___ 8. Although there had been _____ during the Soviet era, it has become an epidemic in the years that followed.
   a. corruption
   b. centralization
   c. economic growth
   d. authoritarianism

___ 9. People all over the world, whether they know it or not, depend on Russian
   a. nuclear reactors.
   b. attitudes toward climate change.
   c. membership in NATO.
   d. oil and gas.

Copyright © Pearson Education, Inc., or its affiliates. All Rights Reserved.

Name _____ Class _____ Date _____

CHAPTER 12 Russia   Test B

Critical Thinking

10. Describe some of Russia's resources and name two challenges to resource development.

_____
_____
_____
_____

11. How did Russia change under the rule of Catherine II?

_____
_____
_____
_____

12. How did Vladimir Putin bring significant improvement to the daily life of Russians during his two terms as president?

_____
_____
_____
_____

Essay

13. Given Russia's geography and history, what opportunities or problems do you predict Russia will face in the rest of this century as it attempts to increase its political and economic power?

_____
_____
_____
_____
_____
_____
_____
_____
_____
_____
_____
_____

Name _____ Class _____ Date _____

CHAPTER 13 West and Central Africa

Test A

Key Terms

Complete each statement.

1. A(n) _____ is a series of flat grasslands with few trees.
2. A life-threatening disease that is carried by mosquitoes, and that is common in the tropical and subtropical regions of Africa is called _____.
3. The Atlantic slave trade began in _____.
4. The trade between West Africans and Arabs that began around A.D. 750 was called the _____.
5. A(n) _____ is a type of West African storyteller who uses music.

Key Ideas

Identify the choice that best completes the statement or answers the question.

____ 6. Due to the different climate zones in Chad, farmers live mostly in the
   a. south, where there is arable land.
   b. north, where they raise camels.
   c. central area, where they raise cattle.
   d. east, where there are cities.

____ 7. The political movement that brought Africans from different countries together in the 1950s was known as
   a. imperialism.
   b. the salt trade.
   c. colonialism.
   d. Pan-Africanism.

____ 8. What is one reason why Nigerians remain poor, despite the fact that their nation has large oil deposits?
   a. Infrastructure
   b. Subsistence farming
   c. Corruption
   d. Microcredit

____ 9. One possible answer to the economic problems in West and Central Africa is
   a. griots.
   b. microcredit.
   c. imports of natural resources.
   d. negative balance of trade.

____ 10. Ghana is thriving more than other nations in the region partly because after Jerry Rawlings seized power in 1981, he
   a. nationalized the oil industry.
   b. abolished the military.
   c. imposed high tariffs on imported goods.
   d. introduced economic reforms.

Name _____ Class _____ Date _____

CHAPTER 13 West and Central Africa

Test A

Critical Thinking

11. What effect does deforestation have on the food supply in West and Central Africa?
_____
_____
_____
_____

12. What are some effects that war has had on people in West and Central Africa?
_____
_____
_____
_____

13. Which natural resources play an important part in helping West and Central African countries build their economies?
_____
_____
_____
_____

Essay

14. How are the problems of poverty and disease that people in West and Central Africa face similar?
_____
_____
_____
_____
_____
_____
_____
_____
_____
_____

Copyright © Pearson Education, Inc., or its affiliates. All Rights Reserved.

Name _____ Class _____ Date _____

CHAPTER 13 West and Central Africa

Test B

Key Terms

Complete each statement.

1. Chad's farmers live mainly in the south because they need _____ land to farm.

2. A fairly dry area between the Sahara desert and the wetter regions to the south is the _____.

3. When trees are cut down faster than new ones grow, _____ occurs.

4. European countries taking over different parts of Africa is an example of _____.

5. The _____ is an organization of African nations that promotes African unity and economic development.

Key Ideas

Identify the choice that best completes the statement or answers the question.

____ 6. The climate along the equator in Africa is
  a. hot and dry.
  b. hot and wet.
  c. wet and dry.
  d. cold and dry.

____ 7. Which African climate zone is home to the savanna?
  a. Tropical wet
  b. Tropical wet and dry
  c. Semiarid
  d. Arid

____ 8. During the period when Arab traders came to West and Central Africa to trade salt for gold, they changed the culture of the region by bringing
  a. the religion of Islam.
  b. technology like the printing press.
  c. a new style of music.
  d. enslaved people to work on the farms.

____ 9. Enslaved Africans traveled across the Atlantic Ocean to America by way of the
  a. middle passage.
  b. salt trade route.
  c. African passage.
  d. African pilgrimage.

____ 10. The cultures of West and Central Africa are mostly based on
  a. traditional culture.
  b. the influence of Islam.
  c. Portuguese customs.
  d. a blending of traditional ways and modern ways.

Name _____ Class _____ Date _____

CHAPTER 13 West and Central Africa

Test B

Critical Thinking

11. How did the early salt trade lead to the growth of cities in West Africa?

12. Why is corruption such a major problem in Nigeria?

13. How does microcredit help the economies of many countries in West and Central Africa?

Essay

14. How are Pan-Africanism and the African Union similar? How are they different?

Name _____ Class _____ Date _____

CHAPTER 14 Southern and Eastern Africa

Test A

Key Terms

Complete each statement.

1. When two of Earth's plates moved away from each other in Africa, the land between them sank down and formed the _____.

2. A famous part of the savanna in Kenya and Tanzania is called the _____.

3. _____ is a term used to describe going on vacation, learning about ways to help the environment, and taking care not to harm the local environment during the trip.

4. Farmers who settled in South Africa's Cape Colony became known as _____, which is the Dutch word for "farmers."

5. People who are native to a region are called _____.

6. The killing of hundreds of thousands of people in Rwanda and Darfur have been called _____, or attempts to destroy a whole people.

Key Ideas

Identify the choice that best completes the statement or answers the question.

____ 7. Southern and Eastern Africa tends to be drier and cooler than West and Central Africa because Southern and Eastern Africa has
   a. more extensive savannas.
   b. higher elevations in most parts.
   c. more biodiversity in the Serengeti Plain.
   d. greater distance to the ocean.

____ 8. Which of the following was spread across western Africa as a result of the Bantu migration?
   a. The Bantu law structure
   b. Religious ideas
   c. Knowledge of iron tools
   d. Trading methods

____ 9. South Africa is home to the _____ groups, who are indigenous, or native, to the region.
   a. Hutu and Tutsi
   b. Kikuyu and Masai
   c. Zulu and Xhosa
   d. Ndebele and Baganda

____ 10. Unstable government holds back economic development most in
   a. Namibia.
   b. Botswana.
   c. Somalia.
   d. South Africa.

Copyright © Pearson Education, Inc., or its affiliates. All Rights Reserved.

Name _____ Class _____ Date _____

CHAPTER 14 Southern and Eastern Africa

Test A

Critical Thinking

11. How might people use the land to make a living in the drier rural parts of the region, such as in Somalia or Namibia?

_____
_____
_____

12. What were some of the steps in early human development and civilization in the region?

_____
_____
_____

13. If a large percentage of a country's people are unable to read, how might that affect the country's economic development?

_____
_____
_____
_____

Essay

14. What are some of the obstacles that South Africa's policy of apartheid created for black South Africans in their lives? How did the end of apartheid affect the nation?

_____
_____
_____
_____
_____
_____
_____
_____
_____
_____

Name _____ Class _____ Date _____

CHAPTER 14 Southern and Eastern Africa

Test B

Key Terms

Complete each statement.

1. Animals that live in Africa's national parks are protected from illegal hunting, or _____.

2. Scientists have found the remains of ancient human beings, or _____, in Eastern Africa.

3. Some Europeans who colonized Africa were _____, believing that their own cultures were superior to any they found in the region.

4. Early trade between Eastern Africa and Arab countries helped create the _____ language, which combines Arabic words and Bantu words.

5. The _____ is a political party that was once outlawed in South Africa during the system of apartheid because it worked for black civil rights.

6. More than one million people in the region die each year from _____, a disease that attacks the immune system.

Key Ideas

Identify the choice that best completes the statement or answers the question.

____ 7. Africa's highest point, or the place with the greatest elevation, is
 a. Victoria Falls.
 b. Lake Assal.
 c. Mount Kenya.
 d. Mount Kilimanjaro.

____ 8. Animals and plants, such as those found in Africa, can become endangered if they are hunted too much or if
 a. they get infected with malaria.
 b. ecotourism spreads into the region.
 c. they live in a rainy climate.
 d. people move into places where the animals live.

____ 9. Which group of foreign traders were the first to become involved in East Africa's slave trade?
 a. Arabs
 b. British
 c. Dutch
 d. Portuguese

____ 10. Where in the region is the majority of the population Christian?
 a. The north
 b. The south
 c. The east
 d. The west

Copyright © Pearson Education, Inc., or its affiliates. All Rights Reserved.

Name _____ Class _____ Date _____

CHAPTER 14
Southern and Eastern Africa

Test B

Critical Thinking

11. What effect does Sudan's lack of water, usable farmland, and other resources have on the country's people?

_____
_____
_____
_____

12. Which actions taken by European countries in their African colonies were harmful to the people of Southern and Eastern Africa? Which actions were helpful?

_____
_____
_____
_____

13. What can you conclude about the government of Zimbabwe, where President Robert Mugabe has been in office for 28 years?

_____
_____
_____
_____

Essay

14. Since apartheid ended in the 1990s, what progress has been made towards achieving equality between ethnic groups in South Africa? What steps still need to be taken?

_____
_____
_____
_____
_____
_____
_____
_____
_____
_____
_____
_____

Copyright © Pearson Education, Inc., or its affiliates. All Rights Reserved.

Name _____ Class _____ Date _____

CHAPTER 15 North Africa Test A

Key Terms

Complete each statement.

1. In a region as dry as the Sahara desert, a(n) _____ is often the only place to find water.

2. A person who wanders from place to place without a permanent home is a(n) _____.

3. The Ancient Egyptians invented a form of writing known as _____.

4. A body of a dead person that has been preserved to prevent it from decaying is a(n) _____.

5. The idea that religion and government should be separate is called _____.

Key Ideas

Identify the choice that best completes the statement or answers the question.

____ 6. Which of the following statements about North Africa's population is true?
   a. Most North Africans live in rural areas like the desert.
   b. More than half of North Africans live in cities.
   c. An equal number of people live in cities and rural areas.
   d. Egypt is the only country in which most people live in cities.

____ 7. In the A.D. 600s, North Africa was conquered by
   a. the Egyptians.
   b. Arab Muslims.
   c. Europeans.
   d. Africans from south of the Sahara.

____ 8. France lost which of its North African colonies to a violent revolution?
   a. Algeria
   b. Egypt
   c. Morocco
   d. Tunisia

____ 9. The largest Christian population in the Middle East are the
   a. Berbers.
   b. Copts.
   c. Rai.
   d. Tamazight.

____ 10. The average life expectancy of its people is one factor used to calculate a country's
   a. gross domestic product.
   b. gross domestic product per capita.
   c. human development index.
   d. literacy rate.

Name _____ Class _____ Date _____

CHAPTER 15
North Africa
Test A

Critical Thinking

11. How has the presence of the Nile River affected Egypt?

_____

_____

_____

12. How are the people of North Africa trying to preserve their environment?

_____

_____

_____

_____

13. How is it possible for Algeria to have a higher GDP than Libya but a lower average income than Libya?

_____

_____

_____

_____

Essay

14. In what ways do successful governments and economies contribute to a better quality of life in North Africa? How do political conflicts and weak economies harm quality of life in the region?

_____

_____

_____

_____

_____

_____

_____

_____

_____

_____

_____

Copyright © Pearson Education, Inc., or its affiliates. All Rights Reserved.

Name _____ Class _____ Date _____

CHAPTER 15 North Africa — Test B

Key Terms
Complete each statement.

1. The flat plain on the seabed where a river meets the sea and deposits its sediment is a(n) _____

2. As a result of _____, cities in North Africa are growing larger as more people move into them.

3. The pharoahs, who were worshipped after their deaths, ruled over ancient Egypt through a government based on religion, or a _____.

4. Gamal Abdel Nasser was an advocate of _____, or the idea that all Arabic-speaking peoples should form a single country.

5. A country's _____ is the total value of all goods and services it produces in a single year.

Key Ideas
Identify the choice that best completes the statement or answers the question.

____ 6. Which of the following statements about Egypt is correct?
   a. About half of Egypt's land is desert.
   b. Egypt has one of the lowest populations in North Africa.
   c. Most people in Egypt live near the Nile River.
   d. Egypt gets much more rainfall than the rest of North Africa.

____ 7. What geographic feature covers most of the region?
   a. The Nile River Valley
   b. The Sahara Desert
   c. The Atlas Mountains
   d. The Libyan Desert

____ 8. During the 1800s, which area of the region was largely colonized by France?
   a. Egypt
   b. Western North Africa
   c. Eastern North Africa
   d. France had no colonies in North Africa.

____ 9. Which of the following statements best describes the pharaohs?
   a. The pharaohs were the elected rulers of Egypt.
   b. The pharaohs were the chief engineers of Egypt.
   c. The pharaohs were kings who were also worshipped as gods.
   d. The pharaohs led a politically divided civilization.

____ 10. Which of the following North African nations is most often considered to be part of the Middle East?
   a. Algeria
   b. Egypt
   c. Nigeria
   d. Indonesia

Copyright © Pearson Education, Inc., or its affiliates. All Rights Reserved.

Name _____ Class _____ Date _____

CHAPTER 15 North Africa   Test B

Critical Thinking

11. Was the building of the Aswan High Dam a good thing or a bad thing for Egypt? Explain your answer.

_____
_____
_____
_____

12. Why did European nations want to colonize North Africa, and what was the result of their efforts?

_____
_____
_____
_____
_____

13. In what ways do religion and politics interact in modern North Africa? Give specific examples.

_____
_____
_____
_____

Essay

14. In what ways has Arab conquest united the peoples of North Africa in the past and present? In what ways has it divided them?

_____
_____
_____
_____
_____
_____
_____
_____
_____
_____

Copyright © Pearson Education, Inc., or its affiliates. All Rights Reserved.

Name _____ Class _____ Date _____

CHAPTER 16
Arabia and Iraq
Test A

Key Terms

Complete each statement.

1. Because they are created from the remains of living things, oil and gas are known as _____.

2. In most countries in the region, Arab Muslims make up more than half the population, which means those people form a(n) _____.

3. Much of Arabia is heavily _____, meaning that most of the population is concentrated in cities, and there are large areas that have few people.

4. _____ is the practice of worshipping only one god.

5. The belief that information contained in holy books should be believed word-for-word is called _____.

6. If a group of people uses violence against innocent civilians for political reasons, that use of violence is an act of _____.

Key Ideas

Identify the choice that best completes the statement or answers the question.

____ 7. Farming is possible in northeastern Iraq because
   a. desalination plants are located there.
   b. the Euphrates River flows through the region.
   c. the region receives some rainfall.
   d. moist air reaches the region from the Red Sea.

____ 8. The Sumerians developed cuneiform writing, which is a type of writing that usually involves
   a. quill pens writing on sheets of wax.
   b. calligraphy and rolls of parchment.
   c. wedge-shaped marks on clay tablets.
   d. the Arabic alphabet and sheets of vellum.

____ 9. During the early 1900s, Britain had a major influence in several countries in the region, including
   a. Syria and Egypt.
   b. Spain and Greece.
   c. Yemen and Persia.
   d. Bahrain and Kuwait.

____ 10. Wahhabism is the name of a branch of Sunni Islam that interprets Islamic scripture literally and
   a. accepts modern interpretations of the Quran.
   b. states that the government should follow Islamic teachings.
   c. teaches that women should drive cars for their husbands and fathers.
   d. believes in attacking Westerners.

Copyright © Pearson Education, Inc., or its affiliates. All Rights Reserved.

Name _____ Class _____ Date _____

CHAPTER 16 Arabia and Iraq — Test A

Critical Thinking

11. Summarize the history of the city of Mecca and its importance to Islam.

_____
_____
_____

12. What might be the effect if Saudi Arabia were to become a constitutional monarchy, like Kuwait, instead of the absolute monarchy that it is?

_____
_____
_____

13. Analyze ways in which the "easy money" from oil sales may have had a negative effect on economic growth in the region.

_____
_____
_____

Essay

14. Evaluate why countries from outside the region try to influence political and economic developments in the region.

_____
_____
_____
_____
_____
_____
_____
_____
_____

Name _____ Class _____ Date _____

CHAPTER 16 Arabia and Iraq — Test B

Key Terms
Complete each statement.

1. In very dry desert areas, people use a process called _____ to remove salt from seawater.

2. A culture that has a written language and in which people fill different types of jobs is known as a(n) _____.

3. Early followers of Muhammad collected the message they believed he had received from God and wrote them down in the _____, which is the holy book of Islam.

4. The willingness to take the risks and make the effort to start a new business is described by the term _____.

5. _____ is a belief that politics and society should follow guidance from Islamic teachings.

6. A concealing and baggy garment traditionally worn by some women in the region is called a(n) _____.

Key Ideas
Identify the choice that best completes the statement or answers the question.

____ 7. Over millions of years, heat and pressure from inside the Earth changed the decaying bodies of living things into
   a. oil and natural gas.
   b. hydrogen and methane.
   c. nitrogen and kerosene.
   d. oxygen and carbon dioxide.

____ 8. Large Shia Muslim populations are mainly found in
   a. Kuwait, Bahrain, and Oman.
   b. Iraq, Saudi Arabia, Bahrain, and Yemen.
   c. Qatar, Yemen, and Kuwait.
   d. Saudi Arabia, Bahrain, and Iraq.

____ 9. During which period did Britain have a large influence on the Iraqi government?
   a. During the Ottoman Period
   b. After World War I
   c. After the Iran-Iraq War
   d. When Saddam Hussein was dictator

____ 10. An example of entrepreneurship is
   a. starting a new business on your own.
   b. investing in locally owned businesses.
   c. hiring foreign workers for jobs citizens do not want.
   d. educating people so they will become better workers.

Copyright © Pearson Education, Inc., or its affiliates. All Rights Reserved.

Name _____ Class _____ Date _____

CHAPTER 16 Arabia and Iraq   Test B

Critical Thinking

11. How has oil production helped the countries in this region? How has it harmed them?
_____
_____
_____
_____

12. Why did some people in Mecca force Muhammad and his followers to leave the city?
_____
_____
_____
_____

13. What might be the effect if Saudi Arabia were to become a constitutional monarchy, like Kuwait, instead of the absolute monarchy that it is?
_____
_____
_____
_____

Essay

14. Evaluate the aspects of modern global culture that have been adopted in the region and some of the aspects of life in which tradition still shapes the lives of people in the region.
_____
_____
_____
_____
_____
_____
_____
_____
_____
_____
_____
_____

Copyright © Pearson Education, Inc., or its affiliates. All Rights Reserved.

Name _____ Class _____ Date _____

CHAPTER 17
Israel and Its Neighbors

Test A

Key Terms
Complete each statement.

1. A region known as the _____ reaches from the coast of the Mediterranean through Iraq to the Persian Gulf.

2. An underground layer of rock or sand where water collects is known as a(n) _____.

3. In the late 1000s, European armies invaded Palestine in a series of religious wars called the _____.

Key Ideas
Identify the choice that best completes the statement or answers the question.

____ 4. The Dead Sea is a significant feature of the region surrounding Israel because the Dead Sea is
   a. the lowest land on the planet.
   b. a large source of fresh water.
   c. on the border of a mountain chain.
   d. in the middle of the Fertile Crescent.

____ 5. In 587 B.C., the Babylonians conquered the Israelite Kingdom of Judah and
   a. renamed the region Judea.
   b. built a temple in Jerusalem.
   c. chose Abraham as their leader.
   d. carried away people from Judah.

____ 6. In Lebanon, the government's constitution requires that its leaders must be
   a. residents of certain cities.
   b. residents of certain provinces.
   c. members of particular political parties.
   d. members of particular religious groups.

____ 7. How has government corruption in some countries in the region harmed people's standard of living?
   a. By weakening the countries' economies
   b. By decreasing the size of the middle class
   c. By discouraging women from getting an education
   d. By limiting access to the countries' mineral resources

____ 8. When the Hamas Party won the 2006 Palestinian parliamentary election, why did that worsen the Palestinians' relationship with Israel?
   a. Hamas wanted to destroy Israel as a country.
   b. Hamas wanted Israel to invade Lebanon.
   c. Hamas wanted to build security barriers to prevent Israeli invasions.
   d. Hamas wanted to elect PLO representatives to Israel's parliament.

Copyright © Pearson Education, Inc., or its affiliates. All Rights Reserved.

Name _____ Class _____ Date _____

CHAPTER 17
Israel and Its Neighbors

Test A

Critical Thinking

9. Why are the region's rivers a source of international conflict?

_____
_____
_____
_____

10. Compare Jewish, Muslim, and Christian beliefs about Abraham, Jesus, and Muhammad. How are the three religious groups' beliefs similar and how are they different?

_____
_____
_____
_____

11. How does the region's position near the oil-rich countries of the Persian Gulf affect the region's economic importance? Explain.

_____
_____
_____
_____

Essay

12. Evaluate the effect that the Jewish Diaspora and Zionism had on the formation of the state of Israel.

_____
_____
_____
_____
_____
_____
_____
_____
_____
_____

Name _____ Class _____ Date _____

CHAPTER 17 Israel and Its Neighbors — Test B

Key Terms
Complete each statement.

1. The far side of a mountain that is dry and receives little rain or snow is called a(n) _____.

2. According to the Bible, Moses, a(n) _____ or messenger of God, was chosen to lead the Jewish people out of Egypt.

3. The political movement whose primary goal was the creation of a Jewish state located in Palestine was known as _____.

Key Ideas
Identify the choice that best completes the statement or answers the question.

_____ 4. Most of the rainfall in this region falls
   a. in central Syria and western Jordan.
   b. in the rift valleys and the desert plateau.
   c. in southeastern Syria and eastern Jordan.
   d. on the highlands and the Mediterranean coast.

_____ 5. Like the Arabs of the West Bank and Gaza Strip, many Israeli Arabs consider themselves to be
   a. Druze.
   b. Lebanese.
   c. Palestinian.
   d. Shia Muslim.

_____ 6. The United Nations' plan to partition, or divide, Palestine led to
   a. the founding of the Jewish movement called Zionism.
   b. the establishment of Palestine as a British mandate.
   c. the scattering of Jewish people, known as the Diaspora.
   d. Israel's declaration of independence as a Jewish state.

_____ 7. After Paul began to preach Christianity to people with non-Jewish backgrounds,
   a. the non-Jewish people introduced Islamic beliefs into Christianity.
   b. non-Jewish Christians became an important minority in the new religion.
   c. the non-Jewish people rejected Christianity and kept their own religions.
   d. Christians with non-Jewish backgrounds gradually began to outnumber Christians with Jewish backgrounds.

_____ 8. Why did fighting in the second Palestinian Intifada die down in 2005?
   a. Israel moved more settlers into the West Bank.
   b. Israel removed its settlers from the Gaza Strip.
   c. Israel agreed to a peace plan with the PLO.
   d. Israel built security barriers around the West Bank and Gaza Strip.

Copyright © Pearson Education, Inc., or its affiliates. All Rights Reserved.

Name _____ Class _____ Date _____

CHAPTER 17 Israel and Its Neighbors

Test B

Critical Thinking

9. Which of Israel's water sources have caused tension with its neighbors? Why?

_____
_____
_____

10. Describe the sequence of events that took place when the Romans took control of Judah.

_____
_____
_____
_____

11. What difference is there between the education given students in Israel and the rest of the region? How does that difference affect people's standard of living?

_____
_____
_____
_____

Essay

12. Evaluate how the religious requirements which Lebanon places on its leaders affect their ability to govern effectively.

_____
_____
_____
_____
_____
_____
_____
_____
_____

Copyright © Pearson Education, Inc., or its affiliates. All Rights Reserved.

Name _____ Class _____ Date _____

CHAPTER 18
Turkey, Iran and Cyprus

Test A

Key Terms
Complete each statement.

1. A narrow body of water that connects two larger bodies of water is known as a(n) _____.

2. In Iran, underground tunnels known as _____ carry water from aquifers in the mountains to villages.

3. The Ottoman empire allowed religious groups to form self-governing religious communities called _____.

4. In Iran, voters elect members of the country's legislature, known as the _____.

Key Ideas
Identify the choice that best completes the statement or answers the question.

_____ 5. Iran's coastal plain has the country's wettest climate because of moist winds
  a. hitting the rain shadow.
  b. striking the Elburz Mountains.
  c. blowing from the Persian Gulf.
  d. blowing from the Gulf of Oman.

_____ 6. Oil is financially important in Iran because
  a. oil purchases are the country's greatest expense.
  b. oil sales are a major part of the country's income.
  c. oil spills have meant expensive environmental clean-up.
  d. oil exploration requires a large part of the country's budget.

_____ 7. The Byzantine empire ended in 1453 when the
  a. Ottomans became caliphs.
  b. Safavids dominated Iran.
  c. Ottomans captured Constantinople.
  d. Sassanians adopted Zoroastrianism.

_____ 8. Why have many highly educated people created a *brain drain* by leaving Iran?
  a. Because of concern about the country's standards of education
  b. Because of a desire for greater economic opportunity and freedom
  c. Because of a desire for a more Islamic environment
  d. Because of concern that the government is too secular

_____ 9. The northern part of Cyprus is controlled by the Turkish military, which invaded the island in 1974 because
  a. the Greek government was supporting a plan to overthrow the government of Cyprus and unite Cyprus with Greece.
  b. it has large offshore oil reserves.
  c. Cyprus was supporting the Kurdish minority in Turkey.
  d. the Turkish navy needed more ports to control nearby shipping lanes.

Copyright © Pearson Education, Inc., or its affiliates. All Rights Reserved.

Name _____ Class _____ Date _____

CHAPTER 18 — Turkey, Iran and Cyprus

Test A

Critical Thinking

10. How did the Persian road system help Persian armies?

11. How did Mustafa Kemal Ataturk modernize Turkey?

12. How are the viewpoints of Turkey's urban and rural population likely to differ regarding the role of women in society? Explain.

Essay

13. Evaluate Turkey's treatment of its Kurdish population in the past and today. Explain how that treatment has affected the Kurds' relationship with the Turkish government.

Copyright © Pearson Education, Inc., or its affiliates. All Rights Reserved.

Name _____ Class _____ Date _____

CHAPTER 18
Turkey, Iran and Cyprus

Test B

Key Terms

Complete each statement.

1. In some areas of Iran, hot, dry winds called _____ blow almost all summer long.

2. Provinces of the Persian empire were ruled by governors called _____.

3. Turkey became a republic under the rule of Mustafa Kemal, who took the name _____, or "Father of the Turks."

4. When a country's army forcefully takes over the government, that event is known as a(n) _____.

Key Ideas

Identify the choice that best completes the statement or answers the question.

____ 5. More than half of Turkey's population lives along the country's coastal plains because
  a. its major cities are located there.
  b. its electric power plants are there.
  c. the sources of fresh water are there.
  d. the climate is milder and wetter there.

____ 6. To help people trade fairly with one another, the Persians
  a. respected local traditions.
  b. sent official tax collectors to each region.
  c. hired craftspeople to decorate their palaces.
  d. created standard weights and measures.

____ 7. Iran's Guardian Council reviews all the country's laws and
  a. allows only those laws that agree with Islamic law.
  b. elects the members of the country's legislature.
  c. selects the top-ranking officials in Iran's military.
  d. determines which religious leaders will head Iran's mosques.

____ 8. Since the 1980s, Turkey's economy has grown rapidly because the government has
  a. increased the farming sector of the economy.
  b. taken a more active role in the industries it runs.
  c. removed trade barriers and increased imports and exports.
  d. increased production of low-cost goods.

____ 9. The island of Cyprus is split between
  a. Greeks in the south and Turks in the north.
  b. Turks in the west and Kurds in the east.
  c. Arabs in the north and Israelis in the south.
  d. A military government in the east and a theocracy in the west.

Copyright © Pearson Education, Inc., or its affiliates. All Rights Reserved.

Name _____ Class _____ Date _____

CHAPTER 18
Turkey, Iran and Cyprus

Test B

Critical Thinking

10. Which country in the region is an important supplier of energy resources? How much of those resources does that country have?

_____
_____
_____
_____

11. How did Muslim Turks influence Turkey's development?

_____
_____
_____
_____

12. Why do some Turks fear that the military might overthrow the AKP government?

_____
_____
_____
_____

Essay

13. Evaluate the effect of the brain drain on Iran's economy, its dependence on oil exports, and the petrochemical industry.

_____
_____
_____
_____
_____
_____
_____
_____
_____
_____

Copyright © Pearson Education, Inc., or its affiliates. All Rights Reserved.

Name _____ Class _____ Date _____

CHAPTER 19: Central Asia and the Caucasus

Test A

Key Terms

Complete each statement.

1. The countries of Central Asia do not border any oceans, so they are known as _____ countries.

2. In Central Asia's dry desert climate, farmers _____ their land to bring water to their crops.

3. A series of trade routes that crossed Central Asia and the Caucasus region was called the _____.

4. The _____, or traders, who traveled the trade routes turned Central Asian cities into important financial centers.

5. When one group controls the results in an election in order to gain power, it is called _____.

Key Ideas

Identify the choice that best completes the statement or answers the question.

____ 6. What is the benefit of herders moving their livestock from summer mountain meadows to lower plains for the winter?
   a. Moving the animals gives them healthful exercise.
   b. The plants on the lower plains are more nutritious.
   c. Moving the animals prevents overgrazing the mountain meadows.
   d. The plants in the mountain meadows become stale after a few months.

____ 7. From the time that Islam first spread through the Arab world, why would it have taken another 100 years for Islam to reach Central Asia?
   a. Islam spread as Arab empires expanded into the region.
   b. Islam converted Christian believers, which took a long time.
   c. Islam spread as Muslim missionaries traveled eastward on the Silk Road.
   d. Islam spread first through the Roman Empire and then into Central Asia.

____ 8. Following independence from the Soviet Union, the president of Uzbekistan began giving speeches in the Uzbek language because
   a. the government made public use of Russian illegal.
   b. the government wanted to emphasize the use of Uzbek.
   c. people in the audience understood Uzbek but not Russian.
   d. he did not want Russian-speakers to understand him.

____ 9. The protests that forced Georgia's president to resign in 2003 were called the Rose Revolution because
   a. the people rose up against the old government.
   b. the new president was named Rose.
   c. political parties in Georgia used differently colored roses as their symbols.
   d. protesters carried roses as a symbol of peace.

Copyright © Pearson Education, Inc., or its affiliates. All Rights Reserved.

Name _____ Class _____ Date _____

CHAPTER 19
Central Asia and the Caucasus

Test A

Critical Thinking

10. Summarize the governmental changes that have occurred in this region between the 1700s and the late 1900s.

11. What are some obstacles countries in this region face in preserving their cultural traditions?

12. How have farmers irrigating their fields changed the Aral Sea, and how has the change in the Aral Sea affected other people in the region?

Essay

13. How might the physical geography of the Caucasus Region have influenced the broad diversity of languages spoken in the region?

Copyright © Pearson Education, Inc., or its affiliates. All Rights Reserved.

Name _____ Class _____ Date _____

CHAPTER 19
Central Asia and the Caucasus

Test B

Key Terms
Complete each statement.

1. A large, flat grassland in the northern part of Kazakhstan is called the _____.

2. The Caucasus Mountains block cold winter winds from entering the region, so the climate in the Caucasus region is milder, or more _____, than it would be if the cold winds blew there.

3. Traders once traveled through Central Asia and the Caucasus region in groups known as _____.

4. In Kyrgyzstan, traditional storytellers, or _____, recite long historical poems.

5. A government that is _____ strictly controls its citizens and is opposed to freedom.

Key Ideas
Identify the choice that best completes the statement or answers the question.

____ 6. There is very little rain in the region, so to water their crops, farmers take water from the
   a. Amu Dar'ya.
   b. Aral Sea.
   c. Black Sea.
   d. Caspian Sea.

____ 7. Why did it upset the region's Muslims when the Soviet Union closed the madrassas?
   a. The region's Muslims received their medical care at the madrassas.
   b. The madrassas were the schools that taught the Islamic religion.
   c. The madrassas applied Islamic law for the Muslim population.
   d. The region's Muslims bought Islamic foods from the madrassas.

____ 8. Which technology traveled from Asia to Europe along the Silk Road?
   a. Agriculture
   b. Papermaking
   c. Iron-making
   d. Irrigation

____ 9. Turkmenistan has one of the most repressive governments in the region. Evidence of repression includes the government's practice of
   a. forbidding the press from criticizing the president.
   b. holding frequent elections without advance notice.
   c. giving extensive power to local leaders, without being sure they are using the power correctly to help people.
   d. strictly obeying its constitution.

Copyright © Pearson Education, Inc., or its affiliates. All Rights Reserved.

Name _____ Class _____ Date _____

CHAPTER 19
Central Asia and the Caucasus

Test B

Critical Thinking

10. How might Kazakhstan's trade relationship with Russia be affected by the new oil export pipeline that Kazakhstan built in China?

_____
_____
_____
_____

11. Although for some Central Asian countries cotton is a big export product, why is cotton a poor choice of crop for this region?

_____
_____
_____
_____

12. Since countries in the region became independent, what challenge do people face in communicating with each other?

_____
_____
_____

Essay

13. What are some of the ways in which invaders such as the Turkic tribes and the Russians have had lasting effects on the region?

_____
_____
_____
_____
_____
_____
_____
_____
_____
_____

Copyright © Pearson Education, Inc., or its affiliates. All Rights Reserved.

Name _____ Class _____ Date _____

CHAPTER 20 South Asia   Test A

Key Terms
Complete each statement.

1. The _____ was once connected to Africa before it broke free and later joined to Africa.

2. Settlements and cities tend to develop in areas of flat land located along rivers, called _____.

3. Society in South Asia was divided into priests, warriors, farmers, and laborers after the _____ was introduced.

4. India has a government chosen by its people, and not based on any religion, so it is a(n) _____.

Key Ideas
Identify the choice that best completes the statement or answers the question.

____ 5. What brings the majority of wet weather to South Asia?
   a. The northwest monsoon from the mountains
   b. The southwest monsoon from the ocean
   c. Snow melting from the Himalayas
   d. Annual flooding of the rivers

____ 6. Achieving nirvana is a goal of
   a. Buddhism.
   b. Hinduism.
   c. Islam.
   d. Jainism.

____ 7. The East India Company, which took control of much of India, was founded by the
   a. British.
   b. Dutch.
   c. Portuguese.
   d. Spanish.

____ 8. Muslims are the largest religious group in
   a. Nepal.
   b. Bangladesh.
   c. India.
   d. Sri Lanka.

____ 9. Which of the following statements is most accurate?
   a. The Himalayas blocked all contact between South Asia and China.
   b. The Himalayas only slowed down contact between South Asia and China.
   c. The Himalayas were not really an obstacle to movement between South Asia and China.
   d. Many people lived in the Himalayas.

Copyright © Pearson Education, Inc., or its affiliates. All Rights Reserved.

Name _____ Class _____ Date _____

CHAPTER 20 South Asia   Test A

Critical Thinking

10. How did India's declaration of independence affect the nations of South Asia?

_____
_____
_____
_____

11. How does the economy of Bangladesh compare to the economy of India?

_____
_____
_____
_____

12. What forms of pollution threaten South Asia today? What are their causes?

_____
_____
_____
_____

Essay

13. How has trade with other nations affected India?

_____
_____
_____
_____
_____
_____
_____
_____
_____
_____
_____
_____
_____
_____

Name _____ Class _____ Date _____

CHAPTER 20 South Asia   Test B

Key Terms
Complete each statement.

1. As a result of the _____, farming was modernized and more food became available.

2. In 1947, concerns about religion led to India being _____, or split into two nations: India, with a mostly Hindu population, and Pakistan, with a mostly Muslim population.

3. India followed a policy of _____ by refusing to choose sides during the Cold War.

4. The Indian film industry is known as _____.

Key Ideas
Identify the choice that best completes the statement or answers the question.

____ 5. How did people from outside the region cross the mountains along the northern borders of South Asia?
   a. By rivers such as the Ganges River
   b. Through gorges like the Khyber Pass
   c. By crossing shorter mountains like the Western Ghats
   d. By crossing the Thar Desert

____ 6. Where do the majority of people in South Asia live?
   a. Along the coasts of the Arabian Sea and Indian Ocean
   b. In the Himalayas around the major mountain passes
   c. In the flood plains around the Ganges and Brahmaputra rivers
   d. In rapidly growing cities scattered throughout the region

____ 7. The Vedas are the holy writings of
   a. Buddhism.
   b. Jainism.
   c. Islam.
   d. Hinduism.

____ 8. The original civilizations of the Indus Valley were greatly changed by the migration of the
   a. Mauryans.
   b. Greeks.
   c. Aryans.
   d. Mughals.

____ 9. In India, the Dalits, once called untouchables, have traditionally faced discrimination because
   a. of their religious beliefs.
   b. they are all women.
   c. of the rules of the caste system.
   d. of their political beliefs.

Copyright © Pearson Education, Inc., or its affiliates. All Rights Reserved.

Name _____ Class _____ Date _____

CHAPTER 20 South Asia — Test B

Critical Thinking

10. How did the arrival of the British affect India?

11. Compare and contrast the governments of India, Pakistan, and Afghanistan.

12. Why is the population of South Asia a concern for the region?

Essay

13. Does South Asia have more economic advantages or disadvantages as the region looks to the future? Give examples.

Name _____ Class _____ Date _____

CHAPTER 21 China and Its Neighbors

Test A

Key Terms

Complete each statement.

1. Farmland that is good for raising crops is known as _____.
2. Nomadic herders must often move their livestock so that they can find grassland and _____ for the animals.
3. The goal of Confucianism is for all people to _____ in society.
4. In the mid-1900s, Taiwan was able to produce goods cheaply because factories there paid low _____ to their workers.
5. To help cut down on pollution, the Chinese government has turned to building dams to produce _____, that is, electricity made from water power.

Key Ideas

Identify the choice that best completes the statement or answers the question.

____ 6. Crops grow well on the North China Plain because the Huang River
   a. forms a barrier to animals that eat crops.
   b. changes weather patterns in the area.
   c. deposits fertile soil after floods.
   d. carries pollution away from the fields.

____ 7. In a command economy, poor planning is likely to lead to
   a. lower prices.
   b. more farms.
   c. reduced consumer spending.
   d. product shortages and waste.

____ 8. What effect did workers' low wages in China and Taiwan have on export sales?
   a. Other countries did not want the low-priced products.
   b. Other countries quickly bought the low-priced products.
   c. Other countries made low-priced products themselves.
   d. Other countries looked for even lower-priced products.

____ 9. Rural parents in China's market economy often can't afford to pay for school, so their children
   a. are urged to attend college.
   b. frequently find high-wage jobs.
   c. often remain illiterate.
   d. tend to move away from cities.

____ 10. After an uprising in which protesters demanded changes to the country's political system, Mongolia's communist leaders
   a. created a new constitution that protects freedom of religion.
   b. outlawed other political parties.
   c. strengthened the role of the army in daily life.
   d. abolished the elected parliament.

Copyright © Pearson Education, Inc., or its affiliates. All Rights Reserved.

Name _____ Class _____ Date _____

CHAPTER 21
China and Its Neighbors

Test A

Critical Thinking

11. Explain why China's government applies the one-child policy to the Han Chinese people and not to other ethnic groups.

_____
_____
_____
_____

12. Explain how the shift from a command economy to a market economy has affected the number of doctors in rural China.

_____
_____
_____
_____

13. Mongolia's main products are livestock and mineral resources. Give one reason why its economy has not grown as quickly as Taiwan's economy.

_____
_____
_____
_____

Essay

14. Evaluate the effectiveness of both a command economy and a market economy in motivating people to work.

_____
_____
_____
_____
_____
_____
_____
_____
_____
_____

Copyright © Pearson Education, Inc., or its affiliates. All Rights Reserved.

Name _____ Class _____ Date _____

CHAPTER 21 China and Its Neighbors

Test B

Key Terms

Complete each statement.

1. About half the people in Mongolia are _____ who tend livestock and do not settle in one place.

2. In northern China, wheat is a _____ crop, the basis of many diets.

3. Fertile soil along the Huang River starts out as a dustlike material called _____.

4. During China's Great Leap Forward, steel production was favored instead of farming, and _____, or shortages of food, resulted.

5. During the years of China's command economy, many services were provided to rural areas and _____, the number of years that people live, increased.

Key Ideas

Identify the choice that best completes the statement or answers the question.

____ 6. Many inventions were first developed under the rule of Chinese dynasties, including
   a. the wheel and matches.
   b. the plow and the printing press.
   c. the cotton gin and the steam engine.
   d. the magnetic compass and gunpowder.

____ 7. What did a Qin emperor build to make China's defenses stronger?
   a. Three Gorges Dam   c. Grand Canal
   b. Great Wall   d. Taipei 101 Building

____ 8. Did the governments of China, Mongolia, or Taiwan change after the 1980s? If so, which changed, and how?
   a. Mongolia and China both set up a second political party.
   b. China's Communist Party allowed new political parties after the Tiananmen Square protests.
   c. Mongolia and Taiwan allowed new political parties to take part in elections.
   d. The governments of China, Mongolia, and Taiwan did not change after the 1980s.

____ 9. Trade with other nations helps a country's economy. Why is it harder for Mongolia to export goods than it is for China and Taiwan?
   a. Mongolia has a command economy and has few goods to export.
   b. Mongolia charges higher export taxes than China and Taiwan.
   c. Mongolia has no seaport, which makes it difficult to transport goods.
   d. Mongolia produces goods of lower quality than China and Taiwan.

____ 10. What does the Three Gorges Dam produce?
   a. Electricity from wind power
   b. Electricity from water power
   c. Electricity from coal
   d. Electricity from natural gas

Copyright © Pearson Education, Inc., or its affiliates. All Rights Reserved.

Name _____ Class _____ Date _____

CHAPTER 21
China and Its Neighbors

Test B

Critical Thinking

11. Summarize the effect that China's climate patterns have on the diet of people in southeastern China, as opposed to those who live in the north.

12. Taiwan exports many products, including chemicals, medicines, and electronics. What types of goods are likely to be Taiwan's biggest imports?

13. The growth of China's economy has caused pollution problems. Explain why the government continues to use coal-fired power plants despite the pollution problems they cause.

Essay

14. Predict how the growth of cities in eastern China will affect China's economy in the future.

Name _____ Class _____ Date _____

CHAPTER 22 Japan and the Koreas

Test A

Key Terms

Complete each statement.

1. Due to the number of people in Japan and the Koreas, there is a _____ of natural resources.

2. In Japan, shoguns granted land rights to _____ in exchange for their support.

3. After World War II, the Japanese government took the form of a _____.

4. North Korea's _____, or government that can take whatever action it wants, is led by Kim Jong-il.

Key Ideas

Identify the choice that best completes the statement or answers the question.

____ 5. Both North and South Korea are _____ countries.
   a. flat
   b. isolated
   c. mountainous
   d. tropical

____ 6. Japan has developed an early warning system to warn people of which natural disaster?
   a. Fires
   b. Typhoons
   c. Floods
   d. Earthquakes

____ 7. One way that the government of Kim Jong-il controls the lives of people who live in North Korea is by
   a. requiring every citizen to vote.
   b. controlling information its people receive from the outside world.
   c. enforcing free trade with other nations.
   d. updating machinery in farms and factories.

____ 8. The border between South Korea and North Korea is referred to as a(n)
   a. demilitarized zone.
   b. peaceful zone.
   c. war zone.
   d. economic zone.

____ 9. One of the economic challenges Japan has faced in recent years is
   a. isolation.
   b. limited government.
   c. unlimited government.
   d. recession.

Copyright © Pearson Education, Inc., or its affiliates. All Rights Reserved.

Name _____ Class _____ Date _____

CHAPTER 22
Japan and the Koreas

Test A

Critical Thinking

10. How did the Meiji Restoration influence events in Japan?

_____

_____

_____

11. What is the difference between the limited government of South Korea and the unlimited government of North Korea?

_____

_____

_____

12. What conclusion can you draw about the government's influence on daily life in North Korea? Explain your reasoning.

_____

_____

_____

Essay

13. How might relations between the governments of North Korea and South Korea be different if North Korea had not invaded South Korea in 1950?

_____

_____

_____

_____

_____

_____

_____

_____

Copyright © Pearson Education, Inc., or its affiliates. All Rights Reserved.

Name _____ Class _____ Date _____

CHAPTER 22 Japan and the Koreas

Test B

Key Terms

Complete each statement.

1. Regular weather events that can cause heavy rain and flooding in Japan are called _____.

2. After World War II, the Koreas, the United States, China, and the Soviet Union became involved in the _____.

3. _____ is a popular religion in Japan that involves worshipping Kami.

4. The leader of North Korea, Kim Jong-il, is considered by many people to be a _____.

Key Ideas

Identify the choice that best completes the statement or answers the question.

____ 5. Trade between Japan and South Korea is based on
   a. output.
   b. interdependence.
   c. comparative advantage.
   d. scarcity.

____ 6. Both Japan and the Koreas have been influenced by
   a. the Tokugawa.
   b. a constitutional monarchy.
   c. Buddhism.
   d. shoguns.

____ 7. The rise of Japan as a military power in the early 1900s can be traced back to
   a. Confucianism.
   b. Hangul.
   c. the Meiji Restoration.
   d. the Korean War.

____ 8. One of the reasons that North Korea has a much weaker economy than South Korea does is that North Korea has
   a. few trade barriers.
   b. a command economy that has been poorly managed.
   c. a military that has been dismantled for the most part.
   d. a comprehensive social support plan for its poor.

____ 9. One of the major problems North Korea presents for other countries is its
   a. frequent natural disasters.
   b. economy.
   c. nuclear program.
   d. aging population.

Copyright © Pearson Education, Inc., or its affiliates. All Rights Reserved.

Name _____ Class _____ Date _____

CHAPTER 22 Japan and the Koreas

Test B

Critical Thinking

10. Why did products made in Japanese factories become popular exports?

11. What factors have made South Korea's government and economy stronger?

12. What conclusions can you draw about North Korean's development of nuclear weapons?

Essay

13. How does the physical geography of the region help North Korea to isolate itself?

Name _____ Class _____ Date _____

CHAPTER 23 Southeast Asia — Test A

Key Terms
Complete each statement.

1. In summer the _____ arrive from over the Indian Ocean, bringing heavy rains.

2. In 2004, an earthquake just west of Sumatra created a huge _____ that greatly damaged the lands of Southeast Asia.

3. When the people of the Khmer Empire harvested more grain than they could use, they became wealthy by selling their _____ rice.

4. Much of Southeast Asia's trade is _____, or sea-based.

5. In Malaysia, Muslims must obey the Islamic legal system while also obeying _____ law.

6. In the Philippines, some Islamic separatists are involved in a rebellion, or _____.

Key Ideas
Identify the choice that best completes the statement or answers the question.

____ 7. The mountain ranges on Southeast Asia's mainland shaped the history of the region because the mountains
   a. separated the mainland from the rest of Asia and isolated early societies.
   b. created a climate that was favorable for growing spices.
   c. blocked the passage of the summer monsoons.
   d. accumulated fertile soil where deltas formed on their peaks.

____ 8. Most of the land of Southeast Asia is
   a. below sea level, so a system of dikes is used to keep it from flooding.
   b. contained in a vast land mass with very few bodies of water.
   c. subject to a desert-like climate.
   d. either part of a peninsula or part of an archipelago.

____ 9. Why was the Strait of Malacca *most* important to international traders?
   a. The strait provided the most direct route between India and China.
   b. The strait provided the only route to Southeast Asia's spice-growing islands.
   c. The strait gave Southeast Asia's gold exporters direct access to shipping.
   d. The strait provided the safest route for shipping fragile products such as ceramics.

____ 10. After the defeat of the Japanese in World War II, the European powers that had colonized much of Southeast Asia
   a. created ASEAN to help their colonies become self-sufficient.
   b. failed to gain control as the colonies became independent nations.
   c. swiftly regained long-term control over their colonies.
   d. invested heavily in factories and plantations.

Copyright © Pearson Education, Inc., or its affiliates. All Rights Reserved.

Name _____ Class _____ Date _____

CHAPTER 23 Southeast Asia — Test A

Critical Thinking

11. Why did the Mongols have difficulty conquering Southeast Asia?

_____
_____
_____
_____

12. In addition to the financial reward it already offers for the birth of new babies, what other steps could the government of Singapore take to guarantee its future financial security?

_____
_____
_____
_____
_____

13. In what way are the governments of Indonesia and Malaysia alike? In what way are they different?

_____
_____
_____
_____

Essay

14. Analyze reasons that Muslim separatists in the Philippines' southern islands may want to set up an independent state.

_____
_____
_____
_____
_____
_____
_____
_____
_____

Name _____ Class _____ Date _____

CHAPTER 23 Southeast Asia — Test B

Key Terms
Complete each statement.

1. Mainland Southeast Asia is a landform almost entirely surrounded by water. This type of landform is known as a/an _____.

2. The equator runs right through the islands of Southeast Asia's _____, so temperatures remain high there all year long.

3. Hurricane-like storms in the Western Pacific are called _____.

4. The people of ancient Cambodia's Khmer civilization irrigated their rice fields with rainwater that they stored in _____.

5. European and Japanese colonial governments replaced Southeast Asia's small farms with large plantations and took advantage of, or _____, the people and resources for profit.

6. Individuals who want to break away from their country may form what is known as a/an _____.

Key Ideas
Identify the choice that best completes the statement or answers the question.

____ 7. The Ring of Fire encircles the Pacific Ocean and includes the Phillipines and parts of Indonesia. It is the location for
   a. plantations and farms specializing in growing peppers.
   b. forests that are prone to forest fires.
   c. a string of volcanoes.
   d. a tropical climate subject to many heat waves.

____ 8. Before 500 B.C., India and China became early trading partners with seagoing merchants from
   a. Srivijaya.   c. Bagan.
   b. Cambodia.   d. Indonesia.

____ 9. In 1954, the French gave up control of their colony in Vietnam, primarily because of
   a. a bloody war for independence fought by Communists under Ho Chi Minh.
   b. the entry of the United States into the war in Vietnam.
   c. invasion by the Japanese.
   d. promises that the new nation would not boycott French goods.

____ 10. Which population and environmental issues are affecting the economy of Indonesia?
   a. Overcrowding and growing drought
   b. Declining population and air pollution
   c. Declining population and water pollution
   d. Overcrowding and destruction of rain forests

Copyright © Pearson Education, Inc., or its affiliates. All Rights Reserved.

Name _____ Class _____ Date _____

CHAPTER 23 Southeast Asia — Test B

Critical Thinking

11. Explain how the large numbers of people moving into the urban areas of Southeast Asia in search of jobs may causes a strain on cities' infrastructures and other aspects of urban life.

_____
_____
_____
_____

12. Summarize the spread of religious beliefs in Southeast Asia.

_____
_____
_____
_____

13. Compare the level of democracy in East Timor with the level of protection and freedom in Laos.

_____
_____
_____
_____

Essay

14. What steps might Indonesia's government take to encourage migration to the outer islands?

_____
_____
_____
_____
_____
_____
_____
_____
_____
_____

Copyright © Pearson Education, Inc., or its affiliates. All Rights Reserved.

Name _____ Class _____ Date _____

CHAPTER 24
Australia and the Pacific

Test A

Key Terms

Complete each statement.

1. Australia's interior, known as _____, has plains and low plateaus.

2. The rock-like material made up of the skeletons of tiny sea creatures forms a(n) _____.

3. People who are native to a region, such as Australia's Aborigines, are known as _____ people.

4. Sometimes local areas, countries, or entire regions go through long periods of extremely dry weather, known as _____.

5. Almost all of Antarctica is covered by a thick layer of ice which is called a(n) _____.

6. The part of Earth's atmosphere that filters out most of the sun's ultraviolet rays is known as the _____.

Key Ideas

Identify the choice that best completes the statement or answers the question.

____ 7. Since most of the Pacific's low islands have poor soil and few mineral or energy resources, they
   a. have relatively large populations.
   b. have relatively small populations.
   c. produce bananas and cacao.
   d. are mainly urban centers.

____ 8. In the mid-1800s, what event played a part in the large increase in British immigration to Australia?
   a. Aborigines moved to the Outback.
   b. British colonists discovered gold.
   c. British colonists were allowed to adopt Aboriginal children.
   d. Captain James Cook described the excellent ranch lands available.

____ 9. Australia is governed by its parliament and an individual chosen by the parliament, who is known as the
   a. monarch.
   b. governor.
   c. president.
   d. prime minister.

____ 10. What divides Antarctica into two regions?
   a. The Ross Sea
   b. The Antarctic Peninsula
   c. The Weddell Sea
   d. The Transantarctic Mountains

Name _____ Class _____ Date _____

CHAPTER 24: Australia and the Pacific

Test A

Critical Thinking

11. How did movement of the Indo-Australian and Pacific plates create New Zealand's North and South islands?

12. How was the way in which the Maori earned a living similar to that of islanders from Melanesia and Micronesia? How was the Maori way different from most other island people?

13. Do you think that Antarctica's high interior plateau is a desert? Explain.

Essay

14. Evaluate the effect of climate change on the island nation of Tuvalu, today and in the future.

Name _____ Class _____ Date _____

CHAPTER 24 Australia and the Pacific — Test B

Key Terms
Complete each statement.

1. Some Polynesian islands are ring-shaped coral islands that surround a body of water, or _____.

2. Long before the arrival of the British, the first people to live in Australia were the _____.

3. Churches sent _____ to the region to spread their religious beliefs.

4. An Australian car factory that uses steel and electricity to create its products is an example of a(n) _____ rather than a primary industry.

5. If there is an important and long-lasting change to a region's average weather, scientists say that the region has had a(n) _____.

6. A large body of ice that moves slowly over the surface of the ground is known as a(n) _____.

Key Ideas
Identify the choice that best completes the statement or answers the question.

____ 7. Easter Island is part of the subregion
   a. Australasia.
   b. Melanesia.
   c. Micronesia.
   d. Polynesia.

____ 8. Which group in Maori society was at the lowest level?
   a. Commoners
   b. Aristocrats
   c. Chiefs
   d. Slaves

____ 9. In the early 1900s, who controlled most of the Pacific islands?
   a. The island nations, which set up independent governments in the Pacific
   b. France, Spain, Great Britain, Japan, and the U.S., which claimed Pacific colonies
   c. The descendents of Australia's prison colony, who conquered the Pacific islands
   d. The Maori, who spread from New Zealand and the Cook Islands to the rest of the Pacific

____ 10. The plants that grow in the Antarctic climate include
   a. ferns and willows.
   b. algae and mosses.
   c. conifers and heather.
   d. deciduous and evergreen shrubs.

Copyright © Pearson Education, Inc., or its affiliates. All Rights Reserved.

Name _____ Class _____ Date _____

CHAPTER 24: Australia and the Pacific

Test B

Short Answer

11. Compare the effect of climate on farming in Australia and New Zealand. How are Australia and New Zealand alike, and how are the two countries different?

_____
_____
_____

12. How did leadership in Maori society differ from leadership in Aborigine society?

_____
_____
_____

13. What are the main obstacles to people living in Antarctica on a permanent basis?

_____
_____
_____
_____

Essay

14. Evaluate the effects that may have resulted from introducing non-native animals, such as rabbits and pigs, into Australia's ecosystems.

_____
_____
_____
_____
_____
_____
_____
_____
_____
_____

Copyright © Pearson Education, Inc., or its affiliates. All Rights Reserved.

Name _____ Class _____ Date _____

Final Test
Survey

Multiple Choice
Identify the choice that best completes the statement or answers the question.

____ 1. What causes the seasons?
   a. Earth moving closer to or further away from the sun as it makes it yearly journey
   b. Changes in the intensity of the sun's energy output
   c. Earth's tilt causing different amounts of light to fall on certain areas at different times
   d. Changes in the core temperature of Earth

____ 2. Time in the region surrounding the Prime Meridian is sometimes called
   a. Prime Time.
   b. London Mean Time.
   c. Global Standard Time.
   d. Universal Time.

____ 3. The _____ on a map allows you to measure the real-world distance between two points on the map's surface.
   a. compass rose
   b. contour lines
   c. scale
   d. topography

____ 4. Which of the following is likely to be found only on a special purpose map?
   a. Boundaries between nations
   b. Oceans
   c. Continents
   d. Streets

____ 5. Geographers use the term *place* to describe which of the following?
   a. The mix of human and nonhuman features at a given location
   b. The altitude of a given position
   c. A specific latitude and longitude
   d. A street address with a zip code

____ 6. The theme of human-environment interaction includes
   a. only ways in which humans harm the environment through pollution.
   b. only natural disasters such as earthquakes and hurricanes.
   c. both how the environment affects humans and how humans affect the environment.
   d. only events that have happened since the Industrial Revolution.

____ 7. It takes 365 1/4 days for the Earth to complete one full _____ around the sun.
   a. rotation
   b. revolution
   c. lunar month
   d. ecliptic

____ 8. Earth completes one _____, or full turn, every 24 hours.
   a. rotation
   b. revolution
   c. lunar month
   d. ecliptic

Copyright © Pearson Education, Inc., or its affiliates. All Rights Reserved.

Name _____ Class _____ Date _____

Final Test
Survey

____ 9. Which of the following describes the Earth's mantle?
   a. A rocky crust containing both mountains and seafloor
   b. Solid and metallic
   c. A mixture of solid and liquid matter
   d. Solid, but so hot that it can flow like a liquid

____ 10. The high latitudes, also known as the _____, get less direct sunlight because the sun is near or below the horizon all year-round.
   a. tropics   c. low latitudes
   b. temperate zones   d. polar zones

____ 11. _____ affects climate by affecting the air temperature near it.
   a. Wind   c. Water
   b. Precipitation d. Current

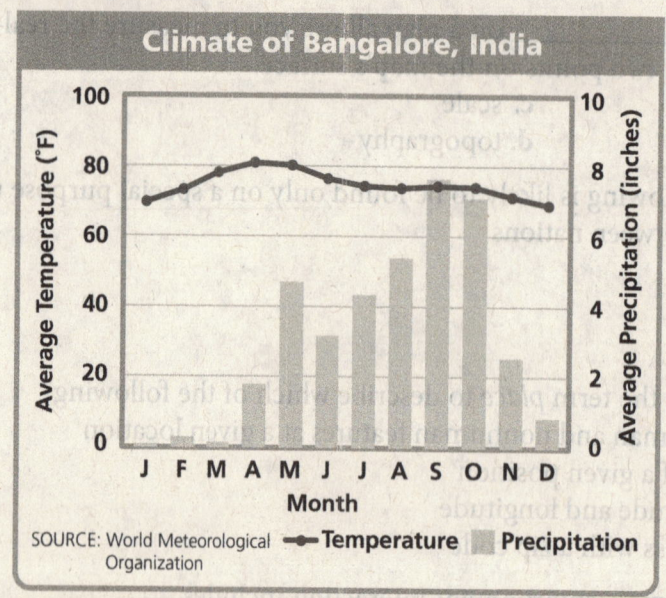

Climate of Bangalore, India

[Graph showing Average Temperature (°F) and Average Precipitation (inches) by Month J F M A M J J A S O N D]

SOURCE: World Meteorological Organization — Temperature ▇ Precipitation

____ 12. According to the graph, precipitation in Bangalore, India
   a. falls mostly from November to April.
   b. falls about the same year-round.
   c. falls as snow in January to March.
   d. falls mostly from May to October.

____ 13. An ecosystem is a network of _____ that depend on one another and their environment for survival.
   a. plants   c. animals
   b. living things d. people

____ 14. The difference between wants and reality creates _____, or having a limited quantity of resources to meet unlimited wants.
   a. supply   c. economy
   b. scarcity d. choices

Copyright © Pearson Education, Inc., or its affiliates. All Rights Reserved.

Name _____ Class _____ Date _____

Final Test
Survey

____ 15. A tariff causes a barrier to free trade because
   a. it is charged at the point of export.
   b. it only applies to services.
   c. it makes the price of a good higher to a consumer.
   d. they can exist even in countries who have joined free-trade zones.

____ 16. A bond is a certificate issued by a company or government promising to
   a. pay back borrowed money with interest.
   b. loan money to the bondholder.
   c. give partial ownership of a company's assets.
   d. share in any profits or losses that occur.

____ 17. Demographers are scientists who study
   a. weather and climate.   c. human populations.
   b. pollution.   d. ocean currents.

____ 18. Using up resources is one of the negative effects of
   a. the birthrate.
   b. the death rate.
   c. the infant mortality rate.
   d. rapid population growth.

____ 19. Scientists believe that more than 50,000 years ago, some early humans migrated from _____ to Asia and then to other continents.
   a. Europe   c. North America
   b. Africa   d. Antarctica

____ 20. The beliefs, customs, practices, and behavior of a particular nation or group is that nation's or group's
   a. norm.   c. cultural landscape.
   b. culture region. d. culture.

____ 21. A set of spoken sounds, written symbols, or hand gestures used by people to communicate is a
   a. culture.   c. language.
   b. society.   d. cultural trait.

____ 22. _____ spread cultural traits because they bring cultural traditions with them to their new homeland.
   a. Traders   c. Migrants
   b. Explorers d. Native Americans

____ 23. Which of the following is a power given to the executive branch of the U.S. government?
   a. Deciding whether a law is constitutional or not
   b. Levying taxes on the citizens of the United States
   c. Conducting the foreign affairs of the United States
   d. Passing laws for the good of the American people

Copyright © Pearson Education, Inc., or its affiliates. All Rights Reserved.

Name _____ Class _____ Date _____

Final Test
Survey

____ 24. Which of the following organizations fights disease by providing food and relief services to victims of war and natural disaster?
   a. Amnesty International
   b. World Health Organization
   c. United Nations
   d. International Red Cross and Red Crescent Movement

____ 25. All political power in the United States comes from
   a. citizens.
   b. interest groups.
   c. political parties.
   d. government.

____ 26.

Column A	Column B
Book	Letter
Movie	Diary
Encyclopedia article	Photograph

In the chart above, what are the items in Column A?
   a. Primary sources
   b. Secondary sources
   c. Artifacts
   d. Biases

____ 27. Which of the following is an example of an artifact?
   a. A toy carved from sticks
   b. A folk-song by an anonymous composer, which old musicians teach to younger musicians
   c. A legend about a hero founding a new city that is passed down by word of mouth, from one generation to another
   d. An old custom that people traditionally follow without knowing the original reason for it

____ 28. _____ is a community's cultural and historical background, passed down in spoken stories and songs.
   a. Archaeology
   b. Oral tradition
   c. Geography
   d. Economics

____ 29. Prior to the American Revolution, most of the large plantations in the colonies were located
   a. near the cities.
   b. in the South.
   c. in the North.
   d. along the coast.

____ 30. Which of these four major regions of the United States was the last to be settled by U.S. citizens?
   a. Northeast
   b. South
   c. Midwest
   d. West

Copyright © Pearson Education, Inc., or its affiliates. All Rights Reserved.

Final Test
Survey

_____ 31. The heartland of Canada, the region where the majority of Canadians live and work, is located
   a. around the Great Lakes and St. Lawrence River.
   b. around Hudson Bay.
   c. along Canada's Atlantic Coast.
   d. near the Arctic Circle.

_____ 32. With which Act did Britain allow religious freedom and French laws?
   a. The Quebec Act
   b. Act of Union
   c. Religious Freedom Act
   d. British North America Act

_____ 33. Agriculture in the Americas began when native peoples began to grow
   a. tobacco.
   b. maize.
   c. cotton.
   d. apple trees.

_____ 34. What is one reason that only about one-fifth of Mexico's land is available to be used for farming?
   a. Because the soil is too damp
   b. Because of a lack of natural resources
   c. Because of mountains, poor soils, and dry climates
   d. Because there are too many rivers in Mexico

_____ 35. An isthmus is
   a. a narrow waterway between two land masses.
   b. a point of land surrounded by water on three sides.
   c. an inlet protected from ocean storms.
   d. a strip of land with water on both sides that connects two larger bodies of land.

_____ 36. In Central America, a hacienda was
   a. a wealthy landowner who controlled the local economy and the votes of peasants living nearby.
   b. the leader of a military rebellion.
   c. a new plan for a government.
   d. a huge farm or ranch.

_____ 37. In 1976, what did the government of Venezuela do to the oil industry?
   a. It installed *caudillos* as leaders.
   b. It sent in paramilitaries.
   c. It introduced austerity measures.
   d. It nationalized the industry.

Copyright © Pearson Education, Inc., or its affiliates. All Rights Reserved.

Name _____ Class _____ Date _____

Final Test
Survey

Economies of Caribbean South America	
Country	GDP per Capita
Colombia	$8,900
Venezuela	$13,500
Guyana	$3,900
Suriname	$8,900

_____ 38. SOURCE: *CIA World Factbook*
According to the table, which country in Caribbean South America has the most productive economy?
a. Colombia c. Guyana
b. Venezuela d. Suriname

_____ 39. What language is spoken by most people in the Andes and Pampas regions?
a. English c. Indigenous languages
b. Spanish d. Italian

_____ 40. Voters in Chile amended the constitution in 1989 because they
a. wanted to bring democracy back to the country.
b. felt a stronger central government was needed.
c. were struggling with a large national debt that was owed to many different foreign countries.
d. needed to clarify the division between church and state.

_____ 41. The Portuguese traded with Native Americans in the Amazon for brazilwood because it
a. was a sturdy building material.
b. could be used in guitars and other musical instruments.
c. repelled water.
d. produced a red dye.

_____ 42. In the late 1800s, which group arose to become the most politically powerful group in Brazil?
a. Sugarcane farmers c. Diamond miners
b. Gold miners d. Coffee farmers

_____ 43. One element of Roman law that still appears in our system of government today is the system of _____, which ensures that no one branch of government becomes too powerful.
a. checks and balances
b. Twelve Tables of laws
c. patricians and plebeians
d. consuls and tribal assemblies

Copyright © Pearson Education, Inc., or its affiliates. All Rights Reserved.

Final Test
Survey

____ 44. Kings granted land to lords, who, in turn, granted land to knights under the system called
 a. manorialism.
 b. the rule of law.
 c. Charlemagne.
 d. feudalism.

____ 45. As feudalism ended and trade increased, Europe found itself in a time of renewed interest in art and learning, called the
 a. Catholic Reformation.
 b. Inquisition.
 c. Renaissance.
 d. Reformation.

____ 46. A book describing the wealth and wonders of Asia, by Italian merchant _____, increased European interest in the riches of Asia.
 a. Henry the Navigator
 b. Marco Polo
 c. Christopher Columbus
 d. Vasco da Gama

____ 47. The four causes of World War I were alliances, nationalism, imperialism, and
 a. communism.
 b. militarism.
 c. fascism.
 d. the Great Depression.

____ 48. Which of the following describes a system of basic services for citizens at every stage of life?
 a. Cradle-to-grave system
 b. Social services benefits
 c. Gross domestic product
 d. Pensions and healthcare

____ 49. What is the European Union?
 a. An international organization that exists to make sure that world war would never happen again
 b. An international organization, also known as the ECC, made up of 6 European countries
 c. An international organization of many countries that works to expand prosperity
 d. An international organization that supports sports teams in many European countries

____ 50. Many immigrants hide from officials in their new country because they fear
 a. immigration.
 b. cultural diffusion.
 c. diversification.
 d. deportation.

____ 51. Which of the following has contributed to Estonia's success in moving beyond the former Soviet Union?
 a. The creation of a large army
 b. Development of an autocratic system of government
 c. Abandoning the Communist economic system in favor of a market economic system
 d. Strict quotas for producing goods

Copyright © Pearson Education, Inc., or its affiliates. All Rights Reserved.

Final Test
Survey

_____ 52. One factor that contributes to the slow economic growth of Ukraine when compared to other countries in the region is
   a. corruption.
   b. available natural resources.
   c. bad weather.
   d. military conflict.

_____ 53. In many areas of northern Russia, a layer of _____ lies beneath the tundra or the taiga.
   a. coal
   b. peat moss
   c. permafrost
   d. ground water

_____ 54. Communism is a political and social system based on a theory under which all forms of industry would be owned by
   a. capitalists.
   b. the people as a whole.
   c. the tsar.
   d. individuals.

_____ 55. One of the ways European colonization upset life in West and Central Africa was by
   a. marketing goods in the area.
   b. splitting tribal groups with borders.
   c. creating friction between Europe's powers.
   d. forcing Africans to not farm.

Money Borrowed for African Infrastructure

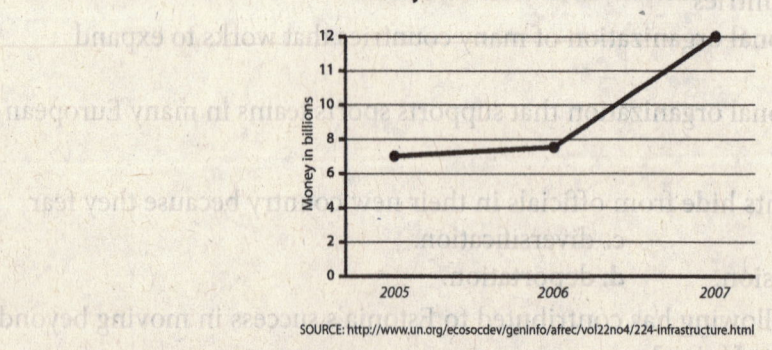

SOURCE: http://www.un.org/ecosocdev/geninfo/afrec/vol22no4/224-infrastructure.html

_____ 56. According to the graph, during this period the nations of Africa borrowed money from other nations, and used it to
   a. increase spending on infrastructure.
   b. expand their military power.
   c. create a social service network.
   d. build a trade surplus.

Final Test
Survey

_____ 57. In the 1940s, British rule in Kenya
   a. was threatened by a German invasion of North Africa.
   b. was established for the first time.
   c. was exchanged for rule by the French.
   d. was being brought to an end by force through the Mau Mau movement of some of the Kikuyu people.

_____ 58. Which African nation has the richest deposits of mineral resources?
   a. Ethiopia
   b. Botswana
   c. South Africa
   d. Zimbabwe

_____ 59. North Africa faces a great environmental problem caused by the erosion of fertile soil, a process known as
   a. pollution.
   b. irrigation.
   c. desertification.
   d. grazing.

_____ 60. Which of the following statements best describes the pharaohs?
   a. The pharaohs were the elected rulers of Egypt.
   b. The pharaohs were the chief engineers of Egypt.
   c. The pharaohs were kings who were also worshipped as gods.
   d. The pharaohs led a politically divided civilization.

_____ 61. Pressure from the Arabian Plate pressing against the Eurasian Plate created
   a. mountains in Iraq and Oman.
   b. fold traps in the African Plate.
   c. the Tigris and Euphrates Rivers.
   d. a broad valley along the shores of the Red Sea.

_____ 62. In Arabic, the meaning of the word "jihad" is a(n)
   a. argument.
   b. struggle.
   c. negotiation.
   d. pilgrimage to Mecca.

_____ 63. Jewish beliefs include following the Ten Commandments, which
   a. explain the customs of religious services.
   b. give instructions for democratic government.
   c. provide guidelines for acting justly and fairly.
   d. give directions for obeying Jewish dietary laws.

_____ 64. Israel is an example of a
   a. theocratic government.
   b. parliamentary democracy.
   c. constitutional monarchy.
   d. authoritarian regime.

Copyright © Pearson Education, Inc., or its affiliates. All Rights Reserved.

Final Test
Survey

_____ 65. Which of the following is an example of how art flourished in the Persian empire?
   a. Large palaces were built and decorated with sculptures and jewels.
   b. Trade was increased greatly in the region.
   c. Taxes were collected in the region.
   d. The Persians built a road system.

_____ 66. Why have many highly educated people created a *brain drain* by leaving Iran?
   a. Because of the oppressive rule of Shah Reza Pahlavi
   b. Because of a desire for greater economic opportunity and freedom
   c. Because of a desire for a more Islamic environment
   d. Because of concern that the government is too secular

_____ 67. When countries in Central Asia and the Caucasus gained independence, they wrote new constitutions, but in some cases citizens in the region still have little freedom because
   a. the countries do not protect the rights listed in their constitutions.
   b. the countries have not established a working government.
   c. the countries are under pressure to promote the economy instead of providing freedom for their citizens.
   d. the countries have been unable to hold elections.

_____ 68. What is the first step that many countries in Central Asia and the Caucasus need to take in order to improve their economies?
   a. Revise the education system to stress use of the local language
   b. Build and improve the country's roads and bridges
   c. Expand contacts with more countries besides Russia
   d. Produce goods to trade on the global market

_____ 69. One way that the mountains of the Himalayas help to regulate the climate of the Indian subcontinent is by
   a. creating a barrier for monsoons.
   b. increasing evaporation as moist air is pushed up the mountainside by winds that blow from the ocean.
   c. blocking cool, dry air from the north.
   d. preventing glaciers from reaching the plains of India.

_____ 70. India and Pakistan have often experienced conflict over
   a. Kashmir.
   b. Nepal.
   c. Sri Lanka.
   d. the Deccan Plateau.

_____ 71. One basis for India's economic strength is growth in industries such as
   a. textiles.
   b. computers and software.
   c. farming.
   d. manufacturing.

Copyright © Pearson Education, Inc., or its affiliates. All Rights Reserved.

Name _____ Class _____ Date _____

Final Test
Survey

____ 72. Which of the following is one of the two major climate patterns in the region near China?
   a. The climate is generally warmer in the north and colder in the south.
   b. The climate is generally colder in the north and warmer in the south.
   c. The climate in the east is drier than the climate in the west.
   d. The climate is generally the same in all areas of the region.

____ 73. In a command economy, which group is in charge of deciding what goods will be produced?
   a. Consumers
   b. Government
   c. Manufacturers
   d. Company employees

____ 74. The physical geography of Japan is best summarized as
   a. desertlike.
   b. filled with broad plains and prairies.
   c. a series of mountainous islands.
   d. a marshy peninsula.

____ 75. Beginning in the 1600s, the Tokugawa shoguns who ruled Japan tried to maintain stability and order by
   a. increasing trade with Europeans.
   b. conquering nearby countries to create barriers to invasion.
   c. developing a new style of writing that was not related to the earlier form of Japanese writing, which had been inspired by Chinese writing.
   d. closing the country off from contact with the outside world to prevent disruption by foreigners.

	North Korea	South Korea
Economic output per person	$1,800	$27,100
Number of phone lines	1.2 million	24 million
Number of cell phones	0	43.5 million
Undernourished people	36%	1.6%
Life Expectancy	72 years	79 years

SOURCE: *CIA World Factbook*, 2008, UN Common Database, 2001

____ 76. According to the chart, economic conditions in South Korea as compared to those in North Korea can best be described as
   a. crippling.
   b. a command economy.
   c. booming.
   d. interdependence.

Copyright © Pearson Education, Inc., or its affiliates. All Rights Reserved.

Name _____ Class _____ Date _____

Final Test
Survey

Ethnicities

Malaysia*
- 50.4%
- 23.7%
- 11%
- 7.1%
- 7.8%

Singapore*
- 76.8%
- 13.9%
- 7.9%
- 1.4%

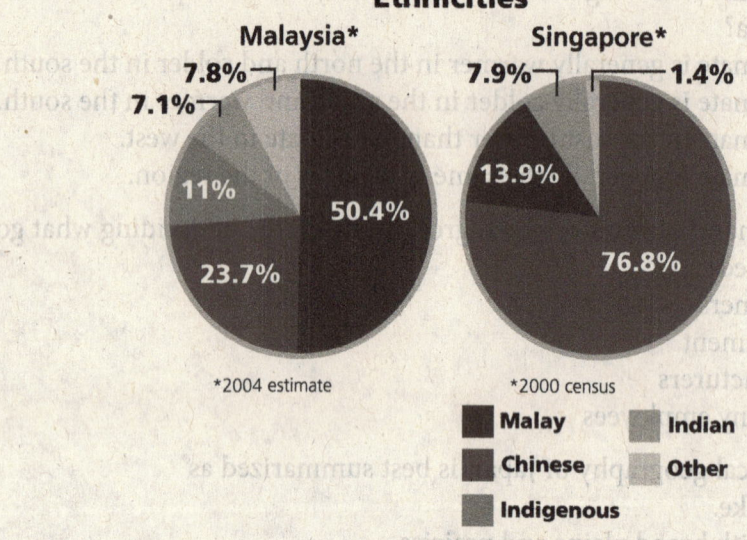

*2004 estimate   *2000 census

- Malay
- Chinese
- Indigenous
- Indian
- Other

SOURCE: CIA World Factbook Online, 2008

____ 77. According to the pie chart, which group makes up about one-fourth of the population of Malaysia and about three-fourths of the population of Singapore?
   a. Chinese
   b. Indian
   c. Indigenous people
   d. Malay

____ 78. When France gave up control of Vietnam in 1954, which group gained control of North Vietnam and which group took charge of South Vietnam?
   a. Cambodian forces gained control of North Vietnam and Laotian forces took charge of South Vietnam.
   b. Communist forces gained control of North Vietnam and non-communist forces took charge of South Vietnam.
   c. Ho Chi Minh's forces gained control of North Vietnam and United States forces took charge of South Vietnam.
   d. Khmer Rouge forces gained control of North Vietnam and Laotian forces took charge of South Vietnam.

____ 79. The early Aborigines were
   a. settled farmers.
   b. settled herders.
   c. nomadic hunter-gatherers.
   d. nomadic fishermen.

____ 80. What forms icebergs?
   a. Blocks of packed ice that stick together
   b. Pieces of glaciers that fall into the sea
   c. Ocean water that freezes in Antarctica's cold climate
   d. Heavy snowfall that freezes on the ocean's surface

Copyright © Pearson Education, Inc., or its affiliates. All Rights Reserved.

Name _____ Class _____ Date _____

Final Test
Survey

Short Answer

81. Compare and contrast Canada's national government with that of the United States.

82. Compare and contrast Mexico's economy in the early 1900s with its economy now.

83. Why were the economies of the newly independent nations of Caribbean South America weak?

84. How did Portuguese colonization change the physical geography of Brazil?

85. What were two Enlightenment ideas that influenced Americans' view of government?

Copyright © Pearson Education, Inc., or its affiliates. All Rights Reserved.

Final Test
Survey

86. How might the viewpoints of larger countries in the European Union differ from the viewpoints of smaller countries?

87. What challenges does Russia face as it finds its place in today's world?

88. What conclusion can you draw about the comparative advantage other countries have in farming over Japan and the Koreas?

89. Compare and contrast the key ideas and development of Hinduism and Buddhism.

90. How did the Muslim Ottomans treat people in their empire who practiced a different religion, and what would have been the probable effect of that treatment?

Final Test
Survey

Essay

91. Explain how wind and water relate to maritime climates.

92. What role do families play in the culture of a society, and how might families either preserve or change culture?

Name _____ Class _____ Date _____

Final Test
Survey

93. Apply your knowledge of the five themes of geography to create a description of your hometown that includes examples of each theme. (You may give your hometown's relative location rather than its absolute location.) How does using each theme improve your description?

_____
_____
_____
_____
_____
_____
_____
_____
_____
_____
_____
_____
_____

94. Would a pure market economy be better than a mixed economy? Explain your answer.

_____
_____
_____
_____
_____
_____
_____
_____
_____
_____
_____
_____
_____

Copyright © Pearson Education, Inc., or its affiliates. All Rights Reserved.

Answer Key

Core Concepts Part 1 Tools of Geography Test A
Key Terms 1. degrees 2. hemisphere 3. aerial photographs, satellite photographs (both acceptable) 4. geographic information systems 5. projections 6. locator map 7. compass rose 8. political map 9. relative location 10. region

Key Ideas 11. C 12. A 13. D

Critical Thinking 14. A map has a flexible scale, can focus in on a single area in greater detail than a globe, and provides clearer labels for roads and other features than an aerial photograph. 15. Measure the distance between the two points on the map, then use the map's scale bar to convert the measured distance into actual distance. 16. Answers will vary. Students should note significant features such as general climate, high or low population, flat or hilly terrain, and so forth. Students should address the geographic theme of place with their descriptions.

Essay 17. Answers will vary.

Core Concepts Part 1 Tools of Geography Test B
Key Terms 1. latitude 2. longitude 3. distortion 4. satellite images 5. key 6. scale bar 7. physical map 8. elevation 9. absolute location 10. movement

Key Ideas 11. B 12. C 13. D

Critical Thinking 14. A globe shows the entire world clearly and in fairly accurate proportions. Maps flatten and distort images. Satellite images show an exact look, which can make it hard to find information. 15. The compass rose provides basic information about cardinal directions that applies to many different types of maps, regardless of the specific information that the maps display. 16. Students should accurately describe the location of their school in relation to another building, using directions and/or distance.

Essay 17. Answers will vary.

Core Concepts Part 2 Our Planet Earth Test A
Key Terms 1. orbit 2. equinox 3. time zones 4. crust 5. erosion 6. plateau 7. plates

Key Ideas 8. A 9. C 10. A 11. D

Critical Thinking 12. Earth's tilt remains the same as it orbits around the sun. This means that at some points during Earth's revolution, the northern hemisphere is tilted more or less directly towards the sun, receiving different amounts of sunlight at different times. These changes in the amount of sunlight cause the temperature to rise or fall, producing the seasons 13. The crust floats on top of the mantle, which is capable of movement. The heat and motion of the mantle act to push up certain portions of Earth's crust. 14. Plains, deltas, and sandy beaches are formed by the deposition of eroded material.

Essay 15. Answers will vary.

Core Concepts Part 2 Our Planet Earth Test B
Key Terms 1. axis 2. solstice 3. core 4. landforms 5. weathering 6. deposition 7. plate tectonics

Key Ideas 8. D 9. B 10. A 11. D

Critical Thinking 12. During each of these periods, one of the hemispheres is tilted closer to the Sun than the other, so they receive different amounts of sunlight and experience opposite seasons from each other 13. There would be no oxygen to breathe, and there would be no layer of gases to trap the sun's energy and keep

Copyright © Pearson Education, Inc., or its affiliates. All Rights Reserved.

Answer Key

Earth warm enough to sustain life. **14.** Mountains, hills, valleys, and plateaus are all shaped by the process of erosion.

Essay 15. Answers will vary.

Core Concepts Part 3 Climates and Ecosystems Test A

Key Terms 1. temperate zones **2.** weather **3.** evaporation **4.** hurricane **5.** savanna **6.** onshore

Key Ideas 7. B **8.** A **9.** D **10.** D

Critical Thinking 11. In the spring and summer, the Earth tilts toward the sun on its axis. As a result, the high latitudes receive more direct sunlight each day than in the fall and winter. In the winter, Earth's axis tilts the high latitudes away from the sun's energy and they get less direct sunlight each day. The temperatures go down. Winters can be bitterly cold. **12.** In the tropics, the sun's heat warms the air. As this warm air rises, it loses its moisture in the form of precipitation. This cooler, drier air is pushed away by the rising warm air. When the cool, dry air is no longer rising, it begins to fall back toward the Earth. When the cool, dry air reaches Earth's surface, it produces winds that blow along the surface and pick up moisture. **13.** Arid climates occur where there are steadily sinking air or winds. In arid climates, the hot, humid air rises, loses its moisture, and is pushed away. The warm, dry air sinks back to Earth's surface. These are the areas where you find hot desert regions.

Essay 14. Answers will vary.

Core Concepts Part 3 Climates and Ecosystems Test B

Key Terms 1. climate **2.** evaporate **3.** intertropical convergence zone (ITCZ) **4.** tornadoes **5.** lose their leaves **6.** semiarid and arid climates

Key Ideas 7. B **8.** B **9.** A **10.** B

Critical Thinking 11. The polar zone or high latitudes, the temperate zones or the middle latitudes, and the tropics or low latitudes are the three zones of latitude. Some zones, such as the tropics and temperate zones, are warmer than others, such as the polar zones, because different areas of the planet receive different amounts of direct sunlight. The different areas of the planet receive different amounts of direct sunlight because of the tilt of the Earth's axis. **12.** As warm air rises, it cools and it loses its moisture as precipitation. The cool air is pushed away, and sinks at the edge of the tropics. It is warmed and rises again in the temperate zones. After cooling and losing its moisture once more, the air falls again at the poles. As a result, precipitation is lightest at the edge of the tropics and then near the poles. **13.** Answers will vary. Possible answer: I think wind is the most important shaper of arid climates because these regions are found where dry air is sinking back to Earth's surface after losing all or most of its moisture.

Essay 14. Answers will vary.

Core Concepts Part 4 Human-Environment Interaction Test A

Key Terms 1. nonrenewable **2.** natural environment **3.** grassland or barren land **4.** deforestation

Key Ideas 5. C **6.** A **7.** B **8.** B **9.** D

Critical Thinking 10. Colonization may impact land use by bringing new crops, new ways of farming, or new animals to a new home. For example, when Europeans colonized parts of Africa, the Americas, and Australia, they often cut down large areas of forest to clear the land for growing crops or feeding their livestock. **11.** Agricultural activities would most likely take place on land used for cropland and grassland. In the United States, there is a large region in the central part of the country that is cropland or grassland. 12. Extracting resources means taking resources out of the ecosystem or the environment. If people take too much of a resource out of an ecosystem, they can harm the ecosystem. For instance, if people cut down too many trees in a forest, they may cause deforestation. If deforestation happens, animals that live in the forest may suffer.

Essay 13. Answers will vary.

Core Concepts Part 4 Human-Environment Interaction Test B

Key Terms 1. environment 2. renewable 3. suburbs 4. spillover

Key Ideas 5. B 6. A 7. D 8. C 9. D

Critical Thinking 10. In some places, large cities grew up around centers for industry. As cities grew, people used land that had been forests, cropland, or pasture, for factories and houses. 11. Natural resources and culture are the two factors that determine how people use land. Land use can be changed by a change in natural resources. Colonization, which is the movement of new settlers into an area, may change the way land is being used. They may cut down trees to clear land for crops and livestock. Industrialization and the growth of suburbs can also change the way land is used. 12. When people use resources to grow food or make other goods and services, they can produce pollution or damage the environment.

Essay 13. Answers will vary.

Core Concepts Part 5 Economics and Geography Test A

Key Terms 1. incentive 2. Demand 3. Profit 4. inflation 5. command economy 6. developed country 7. productivity 8. Exports 9. trade barrier 10. interest 11. stock

Key Ideas 12. C 13. B 14. D

Critical Thinking 15. Consumers buy fewer goods and services, so production slows. 16. The government provides services and money to businesses and households. It receives resources, goods and services, and money in the form of taxes from businesses and households. 17. Improved technology can create new products and make it easier for people to do business, which helps increase development.

Essay 18. Answers will vary.

Core Concepts Part 5 Economic and Geography Test B

Key Terms 1. supply 2. market 3. specialization 4. competition 5. market economy 6. Development 7. Technology 8. Imports 9. free trade 10. Credit 11. Investing

Key Ideas 12. D 13. C 14. A

Critical Thinking 15. Recession can lead to unemployment because when the economy's growth declines, demand decreases as well. As demand decreases, fewer people are needed to produce goods and services, leading to unemployment. 16. Both Japan and Cuba have mixed economies. However, Japan's economy is close to a pure market economy and Cuba's economy is close to a pure command economy. 17. Improving education and training increases workers' skill and knowledge, which gets them higher wages. More people with higher wages leads to increased development.

Essay 18. Answers will vary.

Answer Key

Core Concepts Part 6 Population and Movement Test A

Key Terms 1. birth rate 2. population density 3. internal 4. pull factors 5. slums 6. urbanization 7. suburban

Key Ideas 8. B 9. B 10. B 11. A

Critical Thinking 12. Population can grow faster than the supply of food, water, medicine, and other resources. When this happens, starvation and disease can cause a high infant mortality rate. 13. Immigrants come to the United States for jobs, freedom, the chance for a better life, and other reasons 14. Urbanization is the movement of people from rural areas to urban areas. People who are already residents of the city have their lives disrupted by traffic, pollution, and increasing housing costs.

Essay 15. Answers will vary.

Core Concepts Part 6 Population and Movement Test B

Key Terms 1. death rate 2. infant mortality rate 3. population distribution 4. immigrant 5. living conditions 6. Involuntary 7. sprawl

Key Ideas 8. A 9. D 10. B 11. A

Critical Thinking 12. When the population grows, people use up resources to survive. They cut down forests to get firewood or to open up land for farming. Too much deforestation can lead to the spread of desert-like conditions, which makes it even harder to grow food. Pollution affects the water supply, which can lead to disease and starvation. 13. The population of a country usually increases when the country's birth rate is higher than its death rate. However, if more people move into the country than move out, the country's population will grow. If the difference between the number of people moving into the country is much larger than the number of people leaving the country, the population can increase significantly. 14. Answers will vary. Possible answer: People living in the rural area would be faced with a decision about whether to migrate or not. They might decide to stay where they were and become part of the suburban neighborhood. On the other hand, those people might feel that they were being pushed out of their homes and their way of life. So they might choose to migrate to another rural area, where they could keep the same way of life.

Essay 15. Answers will vary.

Core Concepts Part 7 Culture and Geography Test A

Key Terms 1. cultural landscapes 2. social structure 3. extended 4. third language 5. ethics 6. cultural diffusion

Key Ideas 7. B 8. B 9. B 10. D

Critical Thinking 11. No, political boundaries and culture regions do not have to match. Earth has thousands of different cultures and culture regions. Culture regions may also extend beyond political boundaries. Latin America is an example of several countries that share a common culture. 12. A culture changes when its cultural traits change. Cultural traits develop and change in places called cultural hearths. Then, traits from cultural hearths spread to surrounding cultures and regions. In general, for a new cultural trait to be adopted by a culture, it must offer some benefit or improvement over an existing trait. An improvement will become part of the culture. 13. Refrigeration made it possible to keep food fresh and safe longer than it would have been without refrigeration. Refrigeration made it possible to ship food long distances—from farms to cities—without the food spoiling. Refrigeration also make it possible for people to buy food and keep it until they are ready to use it to eat.

Essay 14. Answers will vary.

Core Concepts Part 7 Culture and Geography Test B
Key Terms 1. norm 2. nuclear 3. ancestor 4. Muslims 5. traditional religions 6. cultural diffusion

Key Ideas 7. D 8. D 9. C 10. A

Critical Thinking 11. Many of the people who live in the countries in this area are Arab Muslims. That means they practice the religion of Islam and they share other cultural traits. They speak the Arabic language, eat similar foods, and share other cultural traits. 12. Possible answer: Cultural change takes time because many people do not want to change the cultural traits they live with. When a new trait enters a culture, some people may adopt it. Other people prefer to do what they have always done. 13. The two vehicles are made from different materials. The chariot was powered by donkeys, but the car is powered by a gasoline engine. The car can go farther and faster than the chariot can. However, the two vehicles are similar in a number of ways: they both have wheels, they are both convertibles, and both are designed to carry people.

Essay 14. Answers will vary.

Core Concepts Part 8 Government and Citizenship Test A
Key Terms 1. constitution 2. unlimited 3. unitary system 4. foreign policy 5. treaty 6. civic participation

Key Ideas 7. A 8. B 9. B 10. D

Critical Thinking 11. Both governments were democracies in which citizens held political power. Athens was a direct democracy in which citizens gathered to pass laws and choose leaders. The United States is a representative democracy where citizens elect representatives who pass laws. 12. The highest institution of the legislative branch is Congress, the highest office of the Executive branch is the President, and the highest institution of the judicial branch is the Supreme Court. Congress makes laws, the executive branch enforces laws, and the Supreme Court interprets laws and decides their constitutionality. Congress also raises taxes and represents the interests of the citizens. The executive branch also conducts foreign policy, manages daily affairs, and provides for national defense. The judicial branch also settles disputes in courts of law. 13. The United Nations is the largest international organization working for peace, with nearly every country in the world sending representatives to the UN to engage in diplomacy. The UN also seeks to protect the rights guaranteed in the UN Declaration of Human Rights.

Essay 14. Answers will vary.

Core Concepts Part 8 Government and Citizenship Test B
Key Terms 1. limited 2. tyranny 3. federal system 4. diplomacy 5. Civic life 6. interest group

Key Ideas 7. B 8. B 9. B 10. D

Critical Thinking 11. In principle, both forms of government provide order and basic services for their citizens. Limited governments use laws to restrict the authority of government actions. They protect their citizens, provide for their needs, and often give them a voice in changing government. Unlimited

Answer Key

governments have no limits on their actions and often fail to protect the basic rights of their citizens. 12. Both are units of government that apply to regions. A state is simply a region that shares a common government. A nation-state is independent of other states. 13. Many international relief organizations, such as the International Red Cross, bring relief to countries and regions suffering from conflict. Countries sign treaties such as the Geneva Convention to try to limit the suffering of soldiers, prisoners, and civilians during wartime. And organizations such as the United Nations try to maintain peace and prevent future conflicts.

Essay 14. Answers will vary.

Core Concepts Part 9 Tools of History Test A

Key Terms 1. timeline 2. prehistory 3. primary source 4. secondary 5. anthropology 6. archaeology 7. historical map

Key Ideas 8. B 9. A 10. C 11. D

Critical Thinking 12. Artifacts would be unlikely to show bias because they were created by people to help them in their lives, not to describe their lives. 13. Historians study primary sources to understand events from the point of view of the people who experienced them. 14. They might not have had writing, so it was important to keep track of a society's events through oral traditions.

Essay 15. Answers will vary.

Core Concepts Part 9 Tools of History Test B

Key Terms 1. historian 2. chronology 3. secondary source 4. primary 5. bias 6. archaeology 7. anthropology

Key Ideas 8. D 9. B 10. D 11. B

Critical Thinking 12. The person creating the source may not remember exactly what happened even though he or she experienced it. Also, the person creating the source may have opinions about the event that lead him or her to leave out or exaggerate information. 13. Answers will vary. Possible answer: An artifact might tell a historian how people in the society got food or celebrated. 14. A historian might learn about significant events in the history of a community, or about what the community values.

Essay 15. Answers will vary.

Chapter 1 The United States Test A

Key Terms 1. temperate 2. export

Key Ideas 3. C 4. B 5. A 6. A 7. B 8. C

Critical Thinking 9. Answers will vary. Students may cite the Rocky Mountains, which cut through a large number of western states and make the area unsuitable for settlement, and the arid climate conditions present throughout much of the Southwest. 10. As U.S. settlers moved westward in order to fulfill their Manifest Destiny, they pushed Native Americans off their own lands. 11. U.S. leaders routinely use diplomacy as a non-violent way to negotiate and discuss economic issues and international conflicts with other nations as part of U.S. foreign policy.

Essay 12. Answers will vary.

Chapter 1 The United States Test B

Key Terms 1. metropolitan areas 2. market economy

Key Ideas 3. A 4. B 5. B 6. B 7. D 8. C

Critical Thinking 9. Both are major mountain ranges in the continental United States. The Appalachians are located in the East and are lower and more rounded than

Answer Key

the tall, rugged western Rocky Mountains. **10.** African Americans were originally brought to North America as enslaved people by European colonists. Over time slavery was outlawed, but African Americans still did not receive full rights under the law. The civil rights movement led to the passage of laws that recognized African Americans as having equal rights. **11.** U.S. citizenship gives additional rights to immigrants, such as the right to vote. Becoming a U.S. citizen may also reflect admiration or appreciation for America and its values.
Essay 12. Answers will vary.

Chapter 2 Canada Test A
Key Terms 1. tundra **2.** permafrost **3.** New France **4.** cultural mosaic
Key Ideas 5. C **6.** C **7.** B **8.** A **9.** B
Critical Thinking 10. Most Canadians live in urban areas, as do most Americans. Canadian and American rural areas have lower population densities. Many Canadian cities are also located near rivers and other bodies of water, as are American cities. **11.** As Canada grew larger with westward expansion, Britain gave more and more governmental duties directly to Canadians. Canada kept ties to Britain, but its growing population and economic power gave it greater influence as its own country. By the time of the Great Depression, Canada was independent and had to rebuild its own economy in order to become a world power. **12.** Answers will vary. Possible answer: Even if Canada had a less skilled workforce, the country would still possess a large store of natural resources such as minerals and timber. Canada would likely still have a successful economy, but not one as diverse or wealthy.

Essay 13. Answers will vary.

Chapter 2 Canada Test B
Key Terms 1. mixing zone **2.** glaciers **3.** dominion **4.** constitutional monarchy
Key Ideas 5. C **6.** A **7.** A **8.** A. **9.** B
Critical Thinking 10. Canada's cities are located in the country's best climate zones. Also, Canada has an advanced economy and many industries, including manufacturing and service industries, which tend to cluster in urban areas. **11.** The Dominion of Canada did not control its own foreign affairs in the same way that the new Canadian government was able to do after 1931, when Britain made Canada fully independent. However, both governments controlled their domestic affairs and both kept strong ties to Britain. **12.** Canada benefits greatly from international trade. One third of its economic activity is made up by exporting natural resources. Trade also benefits Canada by bringing in valued imports.
Essay 13. Answers will vary.

Chapter 3 Mexico Test A
Key Terms 1. altitude **2.** aqueducts **3.** Mexican Revolution **4.** free market
Key Ideas 5. A **6.** B **7.** C **8.** C **9.** C
Critical Thinking 10. Most of Mexico's oil is drilled along the country's Gulf Coast. Oil is important to Mexico because it is one of the world's top oil producers, and oil exports bring in a great deal of money for the nation. **11.** A short-term cause was the rigging of the 1910 presidential election by the former Mexican president. The long-term cause was the poverty of many people in Mexico, who watched a small group of Mexicans grow wealthy, controlling most of the land, while the majority worked for little pay,

Copyright © Pearson Education, Inc., or its affiliates. All Rights Reserved.

Answer Key

had few rights, and struggled to make ends meet. 12. Many poor and young people in Mexico cannot find jobs, and they come to the United States to work. They often send money back to Mexico to support their families. Such remittances provide assistance to many poor families in Mexico and are an important part of Mexico's economy.

Essay 13. Answers will vary.

Chapter 3 Mexico Test B
Key Terms 1. irrigate 2. conquistador 3. Institutional Revolutionary Party 4. remittances

Key Ideas 5. D 6. A 7. B 8. D 9. C

Critical Thinking 10. Baja California is separated from the rest of Mexico by the Gulf of California. Baja California has less fertile land and fewer landform types than the rest of Mexico and is much more narrow. Like northern Mexico, Baja California is very dry. 11. These areas are rich in minerals. Mexico produces more silver than any other country in the world and has large reserves of copper and iron. These resources can be used in Mexican manufacturing or exported to other nations. 12. For the first time since 1929, the Institutional Revolutionary Party lost a presidential election, to a candidate from the National Action Party. Recent victories by PAN candidates suggest that reforms have made Mexico's elections more fair.

Essay 13. Answers will vary.

Chapter 4 Central America and the Caribbean Test A
Key Terms 1. Tourism 2. deforestation 3. Maya 4. Santeria 5. ecotourism

Key Ideas 6. B 7. D 8. C 9. B 10. C

Critical Thinking 11. The encomienda was a legal system under which Spanish officials could tax Native Americans or force them to work. In return, the Spanish were to teach the Native Americans Christianity. 12. Widespread poverty in the region causes people to migrate to North America or Europe. 13. Traditional tourism, such as large luxury resorts, uses large amounts of resources while ecotourism seeks to minimize environmental impact.

Essay 14. Answers will vary.

Chapter 4 Central America and the Caribbean Test B
Key Terms 1. biodiversity 2. encomienda 3. dictatorship 4. microcredit 5. Carnival

Key Ideas 6. D 7. B 8. D 9. B 10. A

Critical Thinking 11. Answers will vary. Possible answer: Some people might think the economic benefits are important. Other people might think the presence of many tourists makes life difficult for local people because it increases population density and can lead to water shortages. 12. Some people might have appreciated the economic benefit and other people might have wanted to be independent of foreign influence. 13. Immigrants send money to support their families. Cultural diffusion occurs when people bring their cultural traits, such as food, music, and beliefs, with them.

Essay 14. Answers will vary.

Chapter 5 Caribbean South America Test A
Key Terms 1. cordilleras 2. *caudillos* 3. austerity measures 4. subsidence 5. insurgents 6. nationalized

Key Ideas 7. C 8. A 9. A 10. D

Answer Key

Critical Thinking 11. Possible answers: European colonists built settlements, established plantations, and dug mines. 12. Landforms divide the region's population unevenly. The Andes, which are mountainous, have smaller populations made up mostly of mestizos and Native Americans. The Pampas, which have many cities, have larger populations whose residents are mostly of Spanish and Italian descent. 13. Because of oil, Venezuela has the strongest economy in the region. Profits from oil fund social programs and allow Venezuela to buy a lot of military equipment from Russia. However, Venezuela's economy is dependent on oil exports.

Essay 14. Answers will vary.

Chapter 5 Caribbean South America Test B

Key Terms 1. ecosystem 2. terraced farming 3. El Dorado 4. paramilitaries 5. representative democracy 6. Latin America

Key Ideas 7. B 8. B 9. B 10. C

Critical Thinking 11. There is a variety of climates as a result of the different altitudes of the mountains, and different crops grow well in different climates. For example, bananas and sugar cane can be grown at lower levels and barley, wheat, and potatoes can be grown at higher levels. 12. Possible answer: Some of the wealthy people with ties to Spain were probably happy with their privileged positions in Caribbean South America and wanted stability maintained by colonial rule. 13. Answers will vary. Possible answer: Guyana may profit from offshore oil. It will probably be able to export more and bring in more income, thus raising people's standard of living.

Essay 14. Answers will vary.

Chapter 6 The Andes and the Pampas Test A

Key Terms 1. subducted 2. El Niño 3. immunity 4. oligarchy 5. diversified economy

Key Ideas 6. B 7. A 8. C 9. B 10. C

Critical Thinking 11. Answers will vary. Possible answer: Buenos Aires has a population of more than 12 million people. It is larger and more densely populated than any other city in the region. Most of the region is not densely populated. 12. Both countries became industrialized after independence. They also elected leaders who promised to redistribute land to the people. Both countries also experienced revolutions during which their leaders were overthrown by the military. 13. European influence is one of the key elements that makes the region culturally diverse. There are many mixed race people in countries such as Chile. The dominant language in the region, Spanish, also comes from Europe. However, Native American influence is also strong, and combines with European influence to form a diverse culture.

Essay 14. Answers will vary.

Chapter 6 The Andes and the Pampas Test B

Key Terms 1. vertical climate zones 2. Altiplano 3. Mestizos 4. mercantilism 5. Bolivia

Key Ideas 6. D 7. C 8. B 9. A 10. D

Critical Thinking 11. The two largest groups of people in the Andes and the Pampas are indigenous people and mestizos. 12. Early civilizations were well-organized and sophisticated because they built villages and cities and they organized trade routes. The Incas were especially sophisticated because they

expanded their civilization into an empire. **13.** Answers will vary. Possible answer: The system of mercantilism was unfair to people living in the South American colonies. It took their natural resources from them and then forced them to buy goods made from those resources, whether they wanted the goods or not.
Essay 14. Answers will vary.

Chapter 7 Brazil Test A
Key Terms 1. Amazon Basin **2.** favelas **3.** export **4.** abolitionists **5.** Ethanol **6.** market economy
Key Ideas 7. C **8.** B **9.** D **10.** C **11.** C
Critical Thinking 12. A tropical climate with direct sun, plenty of rain, and humidity supports Brazil's huge rain forest. **13.** During the sugar boom, sugar exports made sugar cane planters wealthy and they controlled the government. Eventually, coffee became an important export, and coffee planters challenged the sugar planters for control. Coffee planters wanted a republic and, along with abolitionists, they formed a new government. **14.** A benefit to cutting down trees is that it clears land for farms and ranching. Since products such as soybeans, meat, and wood are in great demand around the world, cutting down trees allows Brazil to provide these goods. However, there are several drawbacks to destruction of the rain forest. It is a unique place in the world, and its trees absorb carbon dioxide and produce oxygen needed to breathe. Also, the rain forest provides many natural medicines.
Essay 15. Answers will vary.

Chapter 7 Brazil Test B
Key Terms 1. savanna **2.** canopy **3.** coup **4.** urban planning **5.** boom | bust **6.** social services
Key Ideas 7. D **8.** D **9.** B **10.** A **11.** A
Critical Thinking 12. It is hot and it does not experience great changes in seasons. **13.** Brazil's economy would be strong during a boom period, but when demand and prices for the main export fell, the economy would go into a decline. The boom and bust cycle led Getúlio Vargas to encourage manufacturing, so that Brazil would not be dependent on foreign goods. **14.** Brazil is using ethanol as an alternative fuel for cars. Also, it is starting to do some urban planning to address some of the problems of urban growth. Urban planning has allowed Brazil to create a "green city" that is less harmful to the environment than other cities.
Essay 15. Answers will vary.

Chapter 8 Ancient and Medieval Europe Test A
Key Terms 1. direct democracy **2.** patricians **3.** *Pax Romana* **4.** lords | vassals **5.** Crusades
Key Ideas 6. B **7.** A **8.** C **9.** D
Critical Thinking 10. The ancient Greeks mainly settled in the valleys with fertile soil near the coast. These settlements were often isolated from each other by mountains or bodies of water, so each settlement became an independent town or city. This isolation eventually lead to the formation of city-states. **11.** Charlemagne changed Europe by uniting much of it under his rule, converting many of the people he conquered to Catholicism, reestablishing the rule of law, and promoting education reform with his school at his palace. **12.** Italian cities served as hubs for goods coming into Europe. Ships from Constantinople and other cities in the Middle East arrived loaded with gold, silks, spices, and other products. Traders loaded these goods onto

Answer Key

other ships to send them to other cities in Europe.

Essay 13. Answers will vary.

Chapter 8 Ancient and Medieval Europe Test B

Key Terms 1. city-states 2. philosophy 3. representative 4. Schism 5. economic

Key Ideas 6. C 7. D 8. B 9. B

Critical Thinking 10. In A.D. 312, Roman emperor Constantine I became a Christian. That event—Constantine becoming a Christian—greatly sped up the spread of Christianity in much of Europe. 11. The Christian church sent people across Europe to spread Christianity and gain new members. Gradually, most non-Christians in Europe converted to the Christian religion. As a result, the Christian Church and its teachings were at the center of medieval life all across Europe. 12. The Black Death quickly spread throughout Europe. People from all levels of society died—about 25 million Europeans, by the time the plague ended. Europe faced a labor shortage and a shortage of people with important knowledge and skills. The plague sped up the movement of peasants from manors to the cities. In the cities, those who survived were becoming the new middle class.

Essay 13. Answers will vary.

Chapter 9 Europe in Modern Times Test A

Key Terms 1. perspective 2. northwest passage 3. child labor 4. Treaty of Versailles 5. multinational corporations

Key Ideas 6. A 7. C 8. C 9. A

Critical Thinking 10. Renaissance thinkers questioned religious beliefs and ancient ideas. They used reason and logic to observe and understand the world around them. Enlightenment philosophers used ideas from the Scientific Revolution, especially observation and logic, to study human nature. They wanted to change society and government. 11. Fast, new machines in factories began to do much of the work once done by people in their homes. Trade increased greatly because workers in factories produced far more goods than individual workers ever had. Industrialized nations needed new places to sell these products. Many of these new markets were in European colonies in the Americas and Asia. 12. Adolf Hitler, like many other Germans, believed that Germany had been treated unfairly after the World War I. After Hitler took control of the government, Germany's economy improved. As a result, many Germans accepted Nazi rule.

Essay 13. Answers will vary.

Chapter 9 Europe in Modern Times Test B

Key Terms 1. movable type 2. triangular trade 3. logic and/or reason 4. fascism 5. democracy

Key Ideas 6. D 7. B 8. D 9. D

Critical Thinking 10. The Columbian Exchange was the exchange of plants, animals, foods, diseases, and ideas between the Eastern and Western hemispheres. European ships carried plants, animals, and diseases to the Americas. The explorers brought food plants, animals, and ideas to Europe. 11. Antidemocratic leaders were able to take power in the Soviet Union because the promise of economic wealth shared among all workers under communism was a very appealing promise. In Italy, nationalist pride led to fascism. In the 1920s, fascist Benito Mussolini took power in Italy

Answer Key

because he promised to build a strong Italian empire. **12.** The Cold War divided Europe into two parts. One was Soviet-controlled communist Eastern Europe. The other was democratic Western Europe, mostly allied with the United States.

Essay 13. Answers will vary.

Chapter 10 Western Europe Test A
Key Terms 1. taiga **2.** air pollution **3.** pound **4.** European Union (EU) **5.** Iberian Peninsula **6.** diversify

Key Ideas 7. C **8.** D **9.** B **10.** A

Critical Thinking 11. Western Europe's most heavily populated areas are located within 100 miles of the coast because most of the coastal areas are on the North European Plain, where it is easier to build cities. Furthermore, the ocean provides many opportunities for trade. **12.** The warm water from the Atlantic Ocean warms the air, which brings mild temperatures to regions as far north as Scandinavia. **13.** On the one hand, German culture includes some of the world's finest music, art, poetry, films, and literature. Germans have also been leaders in the study of botany, mathematics, and military technology. On the other hand, modern German culture is colored by the Holocaust in World War II and the excessive nationalism of the Nazis.

Essay 14. Answers will vary.

Chapter 10 Western Europe Test B
Key Terms 1. urban areas **2.** Gross domestic product (GDP) **3.** reunification **4.** neutrality **5.** cultural diffusion **6.** deportation

Key Ideas 7. D **8.** B **9.** B **10.** A

Critical Thinking 11. The Arctic climate is cold and relatively dry. The Arctic tundra is a plant community made up of grasses, mosses, herbs, and low shrubs. The Mediterranean climate has mild, wet winters and warm, dry summers. Mediterranean vegetation is a mix of small trees, woodlands, shrubs, and grasses. **12.** During World War II, Nazis wanted to eliminate any groups that did not meet their idea of what German was. Modern Germany teaches tolerance because of its history and its diverse population. Even so, conflict still happens. Some Germans resent immigrants, especially Turks, because they think that immigrants are changing German culture or are taking jobs from Germans. German leaders, recognizing their past, continue to encourage tolerance and open-mindedness. **13.** Answers will vary. Possible answers: Some of the growth in Southern Europe happened because countries such as Spain replaced dictatorships with more democratic forms of government. Entrepreneurs started businesses, large and small companies began to grow and add employees, and privatization of state-owned businesses lowered prices and made the businesses more competitive. Economic growth was also boosted by modernization. At the same time, many of these countries have been moving from making traditional goods, such as textiles, footwear, and porcelain, to developing a service sector that includes telecommunications, financial services, health care, and tourism.

Essay 14. Answers will vary.

Chapter 11 Eastern Europe Test A
Key Terms 1. ice age **2.** capital **3.** secede

Key Ideas 4. B **5.** C **6.** C **7.** D **8.** B

Critical Thinking 9. Religion was restricted under Soviet rule, but after the breakup of the Soviet Union, religious life

Answer Key

has become more active in Eastern Europe. Now, people have more opportunities to start and join religious organizations. With the fall of the Soviet Union, countries in this region have the chance to return to old traditions. **10.** The Northern European Plain has a shorter growing season than areas farther south. Large farms are not as common in the southern part of this region. Also, there are more people available to work the land. Many crops such as citrus fruits, olives, and grapes grow well in the warm climate. **11.** Most Eastern European countries want to join the European Union because EU membership has economic benefits for its members. Member nations gain access to new trading partners and expanded markets. They also gain more sources for raw materials. Both advantages are important to struggling economies.

Essay 12. Answers will vary.

Chapter 11 Eastern Europe Test B
Key Terms 1. emigrate **2.** acid rain **3.** cuisine

Key Ideas 4. B **5.** C **6.** B **7.** A **8.** C

Critical Thinking 9. In Eastern Europe, the location of factories depends on the location of natural resources. Because oil and gas are in very short supply, many countries import the oil and gas they need for their industries. As a result, countries like Ukraine, Moldova, and Belarus have become dependent on Russia for their oil and gas imports. **10.** Poland and the Baltic nations of Lithuania, Estonia, and Latvia have been economically successful because they have moved to market economies, created democratic governments, and become members of the European Union. **11.** Violent ethnic conflicts broke out in the Balkan nations after 1991, sometimes leading to ethnic cleansing.

These conflicts disrupted the economies of the countries in this region. Dangerous, unstable conditions made trade difficult. In addition, many people were forced from their homes and had to start new lives in different countries.

Essay 12. Answers will vary.

Chapter 12 Russia Test A
Key Terms 1. Kamchatka Peninsula **2.** steppes **3.** Bolsheviks **4.** KGB **5.** superpower

Key Ideas 6. C **7.** D **8.** C **9.** C

Critical Thinking 10. Russia's most densely populated areas are the regions that have a continental climate, both warm summer and cool summer. The combination of good climate and agriculture in this region has led to the growth of many of Russia's major cities. On the other hand, much of eastern Russia—Siberia—has a subarctic climate. This climate, which has long, very cold winters and short summers, does not support agriculture. As a result, population is sparse in Siberia. **11.** To prevent civil war during World War I, when many peasants were drafted into the army, and created unrest in Russia, the Duma forced Tsar Nicholas II to give up his throne. The Duma formed a temporary government in 1917, and in the fall of that year, Vladimir Lenin and his Bolsheviks took power. This takeover is known as the October Revolution. Lenin and the Bolsheviks promised that his system—communism—would relieve poverty and provide all the goods and services that society needed for everyone to share. **12.** Under communism, the Communist Party makes all the political decisions. The government owns most property and makes most economic decisions. The political leadership requires party obedience and values party

Copyright © Pearson Education, Inc., or its affiliates. All Rights Reserved.

Answer Key

discipline. They also want economic security. Under democratic capitalism, the people and their elected officials make the political decisions. In the market, private producers and consumers make most economic decisions. The political leadership values freedom and prosperity.

Essay 13. Answers will vary.

Chapter 12 Russia Test B
Key Terms 1. Siberia 2. tsar 3. soviets 4. collectivization 5. censor

Key Ideas 6. C 7. B 8. A 9. D

Critical Thinking 10. Russia's resources include timber, fishing, hydroelectric power, oil and gas, metal ores and minerals. One challenge to the development of all these resources is the great distances separating the resources from areas where they can be processed, and markets where they are sold. A second challenge to Russia's resource development is the harsh Siberian climate in which many of these resources are found. 11. Where some of her predecessors had sought to westernize Russia, Catherine promoted Russian culture. She transformed St. Petersburg into a Russian cultural center. Catherine also expanded Russia by adding some 200,000 square miles to Russian territory, including much of Ukraine and parts of Poland. 12. Vladimir Putin's economic reforms reduced poverty and led to the emergence of a new middle class, which generally consists of professionals who work in fields related to the global economy. Putin also dramatically expanded Russia's energy industry, exploiting the nation's massive natural resources. As a result, Russia has become a world leader in the production of oil and gas.

Essay 13. Answers will vary.

Chapter 13 West and Central Africa Test A
Key Terms 1. savanna 2. malaria 3. the 1500s 4. salt trade 5. griot

Key Ideas 6. A 7. D 8. C 9. B 10. D

Critical Thinking 11. Deforestation dries out the land, which makes it harder for farmers to grow crops that people can eat. 12. Answers will vary. Possible answers: War in West and Central Africa has led to a rise in the number of child soldiers, an increase in the number of African refugees (people being forced to leave their homes), and increases in poverty and widespread disease. 13. Natural resources such as oil, gold, and water for generating hydroelectric power play a key role in the growth of West and Central African economies.

Essay 14. Answers will vary.

Chapter 13 West and Central Africa Test B
Key Terms 1. arable 2. Sahel 3. deforestation 4. colonialism 5. African Union

Key Ideas 6. B 7. B 8. A 9. A 10. D

Critical Thinking 11. The salt trade led to the rise of powerful trading kingdoms that included large cities. It also led to the blending of cultures as Arab knowledge, law, and religious ideas spread to other parts of the world. 12. The poor management of money by Nigeria's government and the country's large oil business make it tempting for people to use their power for personal gain. 13. The small loans that make up microcredit help people start new businesses, which in turn make the economies of their countries stronger.

Essay 14. Answers will vary.

Answer Key

Chapter 14 Southern and Eastern Africa Test A
Key Terms 1. Great Rift Valley 2. Serengeti Plain 3. Ecotourism 4. Boers 5. indigenous 6. genocide
Key Ideas 7. B 8. C 9. C 10. C
Critical Thinking 11. If the region does not receive enough rain to allow farming, people might bring in water to irrigate the land so that they would be able to farm. Raising cattle and other livestock takes less water than farming, so people might choose to do that instead. 12. Early humans moved around searching for food, and they spread out from Africa to other parts of the world. In this region of Africa, the first civilization began in Nubia around 2000 B.C. Nubia became a trading center and traded goods with its neighbor, Egypt. The Nubian people acquired knowledge and skills from their Egyptian trading partners, including the important technology of iron-making. 13. Answers will vary. Possible answer: Having a large percentage of people who cannot read would harm a country's economic development. People who do not know how to read cannot hold jobs that require reading or writing. The country would lack educated workers who can help the economy grow, such as office workers, business managers, doctors, teachers, and government leaders.
Essay 14. Answers will vary.

Chapter 14 Southern and Eastern Africa Test B
Key Terms 1. poaching 2. fossils 3. ethnocentric 4. Swahili 5. African National Congress (ANC) 6. HIV/AIDS
Key Ideas 7. D 8. D 9. A 10. B
Critical Thinking 11. Without much water or ways to grow crops, and with only oil as a money-earning export, Sudan's people are sometimes faced with famine, or a shortage of food. 12. The harmful actions that European countries took included seizing the land, enslaving people to work the land, sending people to other countries as enslaved people, and having no respect for the different African cultures. Some helpful things the Europeans did were to abolish slavery, to bring modern health care to the region, to build roads and railroads, and to build schools so that African people had access to formal education. 13. Possible answer: Zimbabwe is a dictatorship. Although the country has a constitution and holds elections, one man holding power for 28 years looks very much like corruption.
Essay 14. Answers will vary.

Chapter 15 North Africa Test A
Key Terms 1. oasis 2. nomad 3. hieroglyphics 4. mummy 5. secularism
Key Ideas 6. B 7. B 8. A 9. B 10. C
Critical Thinking 11. The Nile River brings water to a country that is mostly desert. The largest population in North Africa lives in Egypt, near this reliable water supply. 12. The people of North Africa are trying to preserve their environment by combating the process of desertification. They do this by planting trees and other plants at the edge of the desert to hold the soil in place and protect the land from erosion. They also set aside land and keep animals from grazing on it. 13. GDP measures the total economic output of a country. Algeria is a larger country than Libya and has a larger economy. However, Libya has a much smaller population, so it has a higher GDP per capita, meaning that its GDP is spread among fewer people. Thus average

incomes are higher in Libya than in Algeria.

Essay 14. Answers will vary.

Chapter 15 North Africa Test B
Key Terms 1. delta 2. urbanization 3. theocracy 4. Pan-Arabism 5. gross domestic product
Key Ideas 6. C 7. B 8. B 9. C 10. B
Critical Thinking 11. Answers will vary. Possible "a good thing" answer: The Dam provides electricity, stops floods, lets people use water more efficiently, and helps agriculture.

Possible "a bad thing" answer: The Dam ended yearly floods, which increased use of chemical fertilizers, causing water pollution. The Dam also forced many people to move and created a breeding ground for mosquitoes. 12. The European nations wanted access to regional resources and trade routes and to force local rulers to pay debts they owed to Europeans. Britain and France each established significant North African colonies, with the French holding most of North Africa and the British controlling Egypt. However, these colonization efforts led to resistance that led to nationalism and eventually independence as the Europeans were driven out of North African in the 1900s. 13. Answers will vary. Possible answer: In nations with secular governments, such as Egypt and Morocco, there are strong Islamist movements that argue that government should be run according to Islamic law. In Egypt, groups such as the Muslim Brotherhood have pushed for greater democracy and terrorism, while a problem, is less severe. In Algeria, there is a stronger Islamic extremist movement that often resorts to terrorism.

Essay 14. Answers will vary.

Chapter 16 Arabia and Iraq Test A
Key Terms 1. fossil fuels 2. majority 3. urbanized 4. Monotheism 5. fundamentalism 6. terrorism
Key Ideas 7. C 8. C 9. D 10. B
Critical Thinking 11. Mecca was an early oasis, trading center, and religious center. Muhammad is believed to have received messages from God near Mecca and spread the religion of Islam from there. Driven from Mecca by people who did not believe in Islam, Muhammad later returned and made Mecca the Muslim holy city. Muslims travel to Mecca from around the world to worship. 12. The king of Saudi Arabia would no longer have total control of the country, and the country might decide to have an elected parliament to help govern. Citizens of the country would probably be able to vote to elect people to the parliament. Individuals might have greater rights and freedoms than they have under the absolute monarchy. 13. Healthy economic growth for a country depends on natural resources, educating workers, investing in local businesses, and starting up new businesses. Many countries in the region have depended simply on the income from oil sales. They have not bothered to educate their citizens, have invested little money except in the oil industry, and have not encouraged people to take risks and start their own businesses.

Essay 14. Answers will vary.

Chapter 16 Arabia and Iraq Test B
Key Terms 1. desalination 2. civilization 3. Quran 4. entrepreneurship 5. Islamism 6. hijab
Key Ideas 7. A 8. B 9. B 10. A
Critical Thinking 11. Oil production helps countries in the region pay for water

Copyright © Pearson Education, Inc., or its affiliates. All Rights Reserved.

desalination plants, for foreign workers to work in their countries, and for imported food. Oil production has harmed the region's environment by polluting Iraq's rivers, as well as the region's coastlines and soil. 12. Mecca's wealthy residents wanted visitors to continue coming to Mecca because visitors spent money in the town. Most visitors worshipped many gods, and the wealthy residents of Mecca did not want Muhammad to drive the visitors away with his teachings of the single-god religion of Islam. So, the wealthy citizens forced Muhammad to leave instead. 13. The king of Saudi Arabia would no longer have total control of the country, and the country might decide to have an elected parliament to help govern. Citizens of the country would probably be able to vote to elect people to the parliament. Individuals might have greater rights and freedoms than they have under the absolute monarchy.

Essay 14. Answers will vary.

Chapter 17 Israel and Its Neighbors Test A

Key Terms 1. Fertile Crescent 2. aquifer 3. Crusades

Key Ideas 4. A 5. D 6. D 7. A 8. A

Critical Thinking 9. Because the region is so dry, most of the countries rely on the major rivers for a supply of fresh water. Conflict happens when some of the countries feel that other nations are using too much water and leaving too little for them. 10. Followers of Judaism, Islam, and Christianity all regard Abraham as an important prophet. Followers of Islam regard Muhammad as the last, and most important, prophet of God, while followers of Judaism and Christianity do not hold Muhammad to be a prophet. Muslims regard Jesus as a prophet, while Jews do not. Christians regard Jesus as the prophesied messiah and the son of God, while Jews do not. 11. Europe and much of the rest of the world depend on oil exports from the Persian Gulf countries. Because those exports must travel through or around the region, it is extremely important to world trade that conflicts in the region do not slow or stop the flow of oil.

Essay 12. Answers will vary.

Chapter 17 Israel and Its Neighbors Test B

Key Terms 1. rain shadow 2. prophet 3. Zionism

Key Ideas 4. D 5. C 6. D 7. D 8. B

Critical Thinking 9. Israel takes part of its water supply from the Jordan River and has had conflict with the country of Jordan over the use of that water. Also, Palestinians are unhappy that Israel uses water from aquifers under the West Bank because that leaves less water for the Palestinians who live in the West Bank. 10. The Romans outlawed Judaism and taxed the people heavily. Twice the Jews revolted against the Romans. The Romans destroyed the Temple in Jerusalem and killed thousands of Jews. Many Jews left the region and the Romans renamed it as Palestine. 11. Israel has excellent schools and universities, while in the rest of the region, schools are of fairly low quality. Israeli students, male and female, become well-educated and earn a high income. In many other countries of the region, women are discouraged from getting an education at all, and men receive an education that provides low level job skills and leads to a low income.

Essay 12. Answers will vary.

Answer Key

Chapter 18 Turkey, Iran and Cyprus Test A
Key Terms 1. strait 2. qanats 3. milets 4. Majlis
Key Ideas 5. B 6. B 7. C 8. B 9. A
Critical Thinking 10. The roads allowed army generals to send messengers quickly from one army camp to another and to march soldiers quickly from one location to another. Easy communication and troop movements would help the armies defend the empire. 11. Mustafa Kemal Ataturk established Turkey as a republic. To modernize the country, Ataturk separated Turkey's government from religion, gave women more rights, reformed the Turkish language and writing, and ordered that people dress in European clothing rather than traditional Turkish costumes. 12. Possible answer: Urban men and women are likely to see today's women as having roles more nearly equal to men. Women hold jobs in many different occupations in the cities and the country was governed by a female prime minister in the 1990s. Women also wear Western style clothing in urban centers. In rural Turkey, very few women hold jobs outside their homes. Many still wear traditional Middle Eastern clothing rather than adopting Western styles.
Essay 13. Answers will vary.

Chapter 18 Turkey, Iran and Cyprus Test B
Key Terms 1. shamal 2. satraps 3. Ataturk 4. military coup
Key Ideas 5. D 6. D 7. A 8. C 9. A
Critical Thinking 9. Iran has far greater energy resources than either Turkey or Cyprus. Iran's oil reserves are the fifth largest in the world and the country holds 10 percent of the world's natural gas. 10. After the Turks migrated to modern-day Turkey in the 1000s, they spread their language and culture, and gave the country its name. They founded the Ottoman empire, which ruled Turkey and other regions for several Centuries. The Republic of Turkey was founded when the Ottoman empire collapsed. 11. Turkey's army wants the government to be secular, or non religious. The AKP party, which currently runs the government, is more closely connected to Islam than other parties. It has passed laws that secularist Turks object to. In the past, the military has overthrown governments that it saw as too religious. People fear this will happen again.
Essay 12. Answers will vary.

Chapter 19 Central Asia and the Caucasus Test A
Key Terms 1. landlocked 2. irrigate 3. Silk Road 4. merchants 5. election fraud
Key Ideas 6. C 7. A 8. B 9. D
Critical Thinking 10. Between the 1700s and the late 1800s, Russia struggled for control of the Caucasus and Central Asia. When Russia defeated the Ottomans, Persians, and Great Britain, the region came under Russian control. After the communists seized power in Russia in 1917, communist leaders divided the region into eight units called soviets. When the Soviet Union collapsed in 1991, the region's soviet republics became independent. 11. Answers will vary. Possible answer: During the Soviet period, people lost touch with their culture's literature and arts. People may not have time or money to spend learning about the arts or traditions, and the government may have to put its budget into support for the economy instead of the arts. 12. Farmers have taken so much water from the rivers that flow into the Aral Sea that the sea has

Copyright © Pearson Education, Inc., or its affiliates. All Rights Reserved.

Answer Key

shrunk in size. As farmers continue to take water from the rivers, the sea continues to shrink. While the sea shrinks, its water becomes saltier. The increased salt has killed many of the fish, and people who worked in the fishing industry have lost their jobs.

Essay 13. Answers will vary.

Chapter 19 Central Asia and the Caucasus Test B

Key Terms 1. steppe 2. temperate 3. caravans 4. akyn 5. repressive

Key Ideas 6. A 7. B 8. B 9. A

Critical Thinking 10. Answers will vary. Possible answer: Until 2006, the only oil pipelines Kazakhstan had were in Russia. These pipelines gave Russia a lot of control over Kazakhstan's oil exports. Kazakhstan's oil pipeline in China reduces Russia's control and puts Kazakhstan in a stronger position for bargaining with Russia. 11. Farmers in Central Asia have to irrigate their fields to grow crops. Cotton needs a lot of water to grow well. As a result, growing cotton in this region leads to water shortages. 12. Before independence, Russian was the language that everyone had in common. Now that the countries are using local languages instead, minority ethnic groups in each country must learn the language of the majority group. Some countries use more than one official language, so members of some ethnic groups may have to learn two new languages.

Essay 13. Answers will vary.

Chapter 20 South Asia Test A

Key Terms 1. Indian subcontinent 2. flood plains 3. caste system 4. secular democracy

Key Ideas 5. B 6. A 7. A 8. B 9. B

Critical Thinking 10. Religious differences led to the partitioning of India into Pakistan, a primarily Muslim state, and India, a mainly Hindu state. This partition led to ethnic violence, massive migration of Hindus and Muslims from one nation to the other, and contributed to later conflicts between the two nations in the Kashmir region. East Pakistan later became the country of Bangladesh. 11. Bangladesh is a much poorer nation than India, with a less diversified economy that is dependent on textiles. India's economy emphasizes global trade, technology, and providing services through outsourcing. India thus has one of the world's fastest growing economies. 12. Severe air and water pollution are two of the biggest environmental problems that threaten South Asia today. Overpopulation, damming of rivers, growing cities, and the need for more irrigation all contribute to water pollution. Burning down of forests, building of new factories, growing cities, and more cars all contribute to rising air pollution.

Essay 13. Answers will vary.

Chapter 20 South Asia Test B

Key Terms 1. Green Revolution 2. partitioned 3. nonalignment 4. Bollywood

Key Ideas 5. B 6. C 7. D 8. C 9. C

Critical Thinking 10. After establishing trade relations, the East India Company drove out rival European powers and took control of some Indian states. India eventually became a British colony. Its economy became very dependent upon Britain, supplying the British with raw materials and buying British manufactured goods. Eventually Indians forced the British out, using mainly peaceful protest. 11. All three nations are

Copyright © Pearson Education, Inc., or its affiliates. All Rights Reserved.

Answer Key

democracies. However, India has a secular democracy not based on religion while Pakistan has an Islamic republic in which the prime minister must be a Muslim. Afghanistan recently emerged from Islamic rule and now has a constitution. Pakistan and Afghanistan are both less politically stable than India. 12. South Asia has many densely populated areas and very high population growth rates. This puts a great strain on the resources available for the growing number of people, contributing to high levels of poverty, health risks from drinking polluted water and breathing polluted air, and damage to the environment as populations expand.

Essay 13. Answers will vary.

Chapter 21 China and Its Neighbors Test A

Key Terms 1. arable land 2. water 3. act according to their roles 4. wages 5. hydroelectricity

Key Ideas 6. C 7. D 8. B 9. C 10. A

Critical Thinking 11. The policy is strictly enforced in cities. Most Han Chinese live in cities. Most other ethnic groups live in less crowded areas. The government allows some people in rural areas to have more children. This policy helps protect China's cultural heritage. 12. The national government used to pay for medical care for all. Under the command economy, the government would dictate where doctors would go to practice. Now, in a market economy, local governments or private individuals must pay, and small villages may not have enough money. In the market economy, doctors can choose to practice where they want. 13. Taiwan has a large population in cities, which are located close to shipping centers, so there is a cheap labor source as well as a transportation system for goods. Mongolia is landlocked, and has a large rural population. Mongolia does not have the same advantages as Taiwan for transportation and labor.

Essay 14. Answers will vary.

Chapter 21 China and Its Neighbors Test B

Key Terms 1. nomadic herders 2. staple 3. loess 4. famines 5. life expectancy

Key Ideas 6. D 7. B 8. C 9. C 10. B

Critical Thinking 11. Southeastern China is warm and rainy. Its people grow and eat large amounts of rice. In the drier climate of the north, farmers grow wheat instead of rice, and people make the wheat into bread and noodles. 12. Taiwan may need to import raw materials to manufacture its products. Because so little of the country is arable land, and the cities of Taiwan are growing rapidly, Taiwan may also import food. 13. The rapid growth of China's factories requires a lot of energy. Bringing in alternative sources of energy is time-intensive and costly. Shutting down the existing power-plants would cause energy shortages, which in turn would impact China's industries and workers.

Essay 14. Answers will vary.

Chapter 22 Japan and the Koreas Test A

Key Terms 1. scarcity 2. samurai 3. constitutional monarchy 4. unlimited government

Key Ideas 5. C 6. D 7. B 8. A 9. D

Critical Thinking 10. The Meiji Restoration led to Japan becoming a more powerful nation. Japan took control of Korea in 1910 and invaded other countries as well. It also led to Japan's involvement in

Answer Key

World War II, and to the attack on the United States at Pearl Harbor. **11.** The powers of the government of South Korea are limited by law, making it a democratic government. The powers of the government in North Korea are unlimited. Power is held by one leader and the government may take any action it wants, making it a dictatorship. **12.** The government in North Korea makes daily life very hard. The country is isolated, people have no freedoms, and the government controls the flow of information in and out of the country. It also controls religion and the arts, and punishes people who disagree with its positions.

Essay 13. Answers will vary.

Chapter 22 Japan and the Koreas Test B
Key Terms 1. typhoons **2.** Korean War **3.** Shinto **4.** dictator
Key Ideas 5. B **6.** C **7.** C **8.** B **9.** C
Critical Thinking 10. Answers will vary. Possible answer: Japanese products became popular exports because they were of higher quality than similar products made in other countries. Japan's modern factories and educated workforce also helped produce goods more quickly and efficiently. This allowed products to be offered at equal or lower prices than similar products in other countries. **11.** South Korea's government has been made stronger by a limited government that has a constitution and gives people more rights. Its economy has been made stronger by government support for companies, improving the education system, and exporting goods like cell phones and computers to other countries. **12.** Answers will vary. Possible answer: One conclusion is that the North Korean government cannot be trusted. It continues to develop nuclear weapons despite earlier promises to stop. Additionally, the government does not seem to care if it harms relations with other countries over the issue of nuclear weapons.

Essay 13. Answers will vary.

Chapter 23 Southeast Asia Test A
Key Terms 1. monsoons **2.** tsunami **3.** surplus **4.** maritime **5.** secular **6.** insurgency
Key Ideas 7. A. **8.** D. **9.** A. **10.** B.
Critical Thinking 11. Answers will vary. Possible answers: The tropical heat and humidity were uncomfortable for the Mongol invaders, who were accustomed to the drier, cooler climates of Mongolia and China. The heat may have caused them to become ill. Also, the Southeast Asian practice of using elephants in warfare took the Mongols by surprise. The elephants attacked the Mongol soldiers. **12.** Answers will vary. Possible answer: The government might raise sales taxes or offer financial immigration incentives for people to move to Singapore from other countries. **13.** Both governments provide their people with a certain degree of democracy. They differ in that the Indonesian government is a republic, which has legislative, executive, and judicial branches. Malaysia, on the other hand, is governed as a constitutional monarchy, with one person ruling as head of state.

Essay 14. Answers will vary.

Chapter 23 Southeast Asia Test B
Key Terms 1. peninsula **2.** archipelago **3.** typhoons **4.** reservoirs **5.** exploited **6.** separatist group
Key Ideas 7. C **8.** D **9.** A **10.** D

Answer Key

Critical Thinking 11. A large, rapid growth in a city's population often means that there are not enough places for people to live. The city may struggle to supply clean water, sewage services, and electricity for its expanded population. There may not be enough doctors or hospital facilities to care for the city's residents and outbreaks of illness may become epidemics. The increased traffic may cause overcrowding on the streets and an increased level of air pollution. 12. The spread of religious beliefs began as traders from India and Sri Lanka brought Hinduism and Buddhism to the region. Chinese traders arrived with Confucian teachings. Later traders and missionaries brought the teachings of Islam and Christianity. Today Buddhism is the dominant religion on most of the mainland, while Islam is the dominant religion on the islands. Indonesia has the greatest Muslim population. The Philippines are largely Christian; the country's Islamic separatists seek to break away and form their own state. 13. East Timor is a republic, and its constitution provides the country's citizens with some protections and freedoms. Laos is a communist one-party state that does not grant its people personal freedoms or protections.

Essay 14. Answers will vary.

Chapter 24 Australia and the Pacific Test A

Key Terms 1. the Outback 2. coral reef 3. indigenous 4. drought 5. ice sheet 6. ozone layer

Key Ideas 7. B 8. B 9. D 10. B

Critical Thinking 11. As the Indo-Australian and Pacific plates collided over many years, the collisions pushed the ocean floor above the surface of the ocean, creating volcanoes and islands. New Zealand's North and South islands were two of the islands created. 12. The Maori and the peoples of Melanesia and Micronesia practiced farming. They grew crops for food in addition to fishing and hunting, while most other island people depended on fishing for their food supply. 13. Yes, the continent's interior plateau is a desert, because it gets less than two inches of precipitation per year.

Essay 14. Answers will vary.

Chapter 24 Australia and the Pacific Test B

Key Terms 1. atolls 2. aborigines 3. missionaries 4. secondary industry 5. climate change 6. glacier

Key Ideas 7. D 8. D 9. B 10. B

Critical Thinking 11. Australia and New Zealand are alike in that both countries have lots of ranches and large farms. Climate makes farming easier in New Zealand than in Australia, because New Zealand's mild, wet climate provides plenty of rainfall. Parts of Australia have a dry season as well as a wet season and much of the continent has a dry, desert climate. 12. The Maori were led by chiefs, and the role of chief was passed down from father to son. The Aborigines' society did not have chiefs or other formal leaders. 13. The extremely cold and dry climate make human settlement unlikely because it is impossible to farm crops or raise livestock. The pack ice makes shipping very difficult or impossible for much of the year. Building materials would have to be imported, as there are no trees. The severe cold prevents outdoor activities.

Essay 14. Answers will vary.

Answer Key

Final Test
Multiple Choice 1. C 2. D 3. C 4. D 5. A 6. C 7. B 8. A 9. D 10. D 11. C 12. D 13. B 14. B 15. C 16. A 17. C 18. D 19. B 20. D 21. C 22. C 23. C 24. D 25. A 26. B 27. A 28. B 29. B 30. D 31. A 32. A 33. B 34. C 35. D 36. D 37. D 38. B 39. B 40. A 41. D 42. D 43. A 44. D 45. C 46. B 47. B 48. A 49. C 50. D 51. C 52. A 53. C 54. B 55. B 56. A 57. D 58. C 59. C 60. C 61. A 62. B 63. B 64. C 65. A 66. B 67. A 68. B 69. C 70. A 71. B 72. B 73. B 74. C 75. D 76. C 77. A 78. B 79. C 80. B

Short Answer 81. Both federal governments have officials with separate legislative, executive, and judicial powers. Like the United States, Canada has a federal government where the central government oversees a collection of local governments. Unlike the United States, Canada has strong ties to the British government and uses a parliamentary system in which the legislative branch elects the head of the executive branch. 82. Free market reforms have opened up Mexico's economy and led to greater growth. Mexican workers once worked mainly in agriculture, but now a majority work in service industries and manufacturing. Foreign investment has increased, as have trading ties with the United States. However, many Mexicans remain poor, especially farmers. Oil remains an important resource for Mexico. 83. These economies were based on the export of just one or two products, and when world prices for these products fell, it hurt the economy in the new nations of Caribbean South America. 84. The Portuguese colonists built settlements in Brazil. They also established sugar cane and coffee plantations and dug mines to extract minerals. 85. Answers will vary. Possible answers: One Enlightenment idea that influenced American government was that individuals are born with certain rights, such as life, liberty, and property. Another idea was that the powers of government belong to the people. The people must consent, or give their permission, to be governed. 86. Larger countries, such as Germany and France, may believe that they have more influence on the policies and laws adopted by the EU. On the other hand, smaller countries may benefit from some of the EU's economic and trade policies. They may want different terms in EU trade agreements than larger countries want. 87. Some of Russia's challenges include improving the standards of living of Russian citizens. Alcoholism remains a major problem, and the rates of tuberculosis and HIV/AIDS are very high. All of these problems are indications of the impact of the social and economic upheavals of the 1990s, and they remain problems to be solved. 88. The comparative advantage other countries have in farming hurts Japan and the Koreas. Since other countries can produce farm goods at a lower cost, and there is little farmland in the region, Japan and the Koreas must import food. 89. Both Hinduism and Buddhism arose in India. Both religions accept the concept of reincarnation. Hinduism came first and influenced the development of Buddhism, which unlike Hinduism was spread throughout Asia. Hinduism has a universal spirit that takes form in many gods. 90. The Ottomans allowed people to keep their own religions and organized religious groups into self-governing communities with their own laws and leaders. Jews and Christians were allowed to hold positions in the empire's government. Granting this kind of religious freedom probably led people to respect the Ottomans and to feel some loyalty to the empire.

Essay 91. Maritime climates are found only along coastal areas, next to oceans or seas. As a result, they are moist year-round. Because water warms and cools more slowly than the nearby land, winds that blow from the water onto the shore cool the land a little in summer and warm the land a little in winter. This effect makes the maritime climate milder than climates further inland at the same latitude. Also, wind plays a part in creating the Gulf Stream and the North Atlantic Current, which bring a mild maritime climate to parts of Western Europe that would otherwise have a colder and harsher climate. 92. Within any society, the family is the most basic unit. Parents and other adults teach children the culture—all the cultural traits—of the society. As long as parents and other adults pass on the cultural traits of the society without any changes, their culture is preserved. As long as people in the society see no benefit in changing cultural traits, families pass on the next generation the cultural traits they have learned, and the culture is preserved. Today, however, people may learn new cultural traits from the mass media, the Internet, by traveling, from immigrants moving to their society, or by migrating themselves to a new homeland. If one individual, or a few individuals, see a new or different cultural trait as an improvement to they way they do things now, they may change. If the change is accepted by more people, the society may change. 93. Answer will vary. Students should be able to give a general description of the location of their hometown, relative to other major cities or features such as oceans, mountains, and rivers. For the theme of place, students can identify key features of the local population, climate, and industry or agriculture. For the theme of region, students should be able to place their hometown in national region such as the South, Mountain West, Midwest, or Northeast, or at least within a larger area such as the western hemisphere or North America. For movement, students should name any major roads carrying people through their community, list any key exports or imports, and note movements of people such as tourists or immigrants who helped build a community. For human-environment interaction, students have a wide range of possible examples. They might consider how the weather or nearby geographical features such mountains or the ocean affect the lifestyles of people in their hometown. They could give examples of how their community affects the local environment in positive or negative ways. For the conclusion, students should focus on the fact that using all five themes provides a more thorough and complete description of their community than would be possible if any single theme were left out. 94. Answers will vary. Possible answer: No, because the government in a mixed economy can provide some support: providing jobs, influencing growth, and protecting consumers, for example. Most countries have mixed economies because a pure market economy would not serve all its people best.